I0795323

Mrs. Slater in the CONFEDERATE SECRET SERVICE

Mrs. Slater in the CONFEDERATE SECRET SERVICE

The Clandestine Mission that Killed Abraham Lincoln

TODD HOLBROOK

EVENING POST BOOKS
Our Accent Is Southern!

Published by Evening Post Books
Charleston, South Carolina

Copyright © 2021 by Todd Holbrook
All rights reserved.
First edition

Editor: John M. Burbage
Design and composition: Kim Scott/Bumpy Design
Cover photo: [Unidentified woman, possibly a nurse, during the Civil War] / Brady's National Photographic Galleries; Library of Congress LOT 6286, p. 10

No part of this book may be reproduced or transmitted in any form or by any means, electronic or mechanical, including photocopying, recording or by information storage and retrieval system—except by a reviewer who may quote brief passages in a review to be printed in a magazine, newspaper, or on the web—without permission in writing from the publisher. For information, please contact the publisher.

First printing 2020
Printed in the United States of America

A CIP catalog record for this book has been applied for from the Library of Congress.

ISBN: 978-1-929647-54-5

This story is told for all of my father's great grandchildren
and in memory of my sister, Carolyn Denise Holbrook,
who in her own way, was as bold and daring as any good spy.

Contents

Preface ix

CHAPTER ONE
A Falling Star 1

CHAPTER TWO
The Making of a Spy 14

CHAPTER THREE
Richmond and Back. 24

CHAPTER FOUR
The Conspirators 32

CHAPTER FIVE
Deo Vindice 47

CHAPTER SIX
Richmond and Back. 56

CHAPTER SEVEN
Courage and Corruption 64

CHAPTER EIGHT
Mission Like No Other 69

CHAPTER NINE
Women on the Brain 76

CHAPTER TEN
Change of Plans. 89

CHAPTER ELEVEN
Elmira, New York 96

CHAPTER TWELVE
"Played for Mr. P" 106

CHAPTER THIRTEEN
Person of Interest 112

CHAPTER FOURTEEN
War of Words 121

CHAPTER FIFTEEN
Jury of Peers 134

CHAPTER SIXTEEN
War Under the Black Flag 142

EPILOGUE
Mrs. Spencer 157

Preface

JOHN WILKES BOOTH, 26, loved acting—especially his own acting. The handsome Marylander of a prominent theatrical family debuted as a child in Baltimore and rose to stardom on stages North and South. But he had a dark side: He was an angry Southern sympathizer in the waning days of the Civil War and—ever the narcissist—brooded over his failure to answer the call to arms and experience the glory of war.

Booth blamed his mother for this, saying she talked him out of signing up for the fight. But the truth was deeper: John Wilkes Booth loved John Wilkes Booth more than anything else, and in his mind he was destined to be more than a mere soldier.

In September 1864, Confederate losses of fighting men and materiel were dire. Maryland was under martial law, and the likely re-election of President Abraham Lincoln—"King Abraham," as Booth called him—threatened to free the slaves on both sides of the Mason-Dixon Line. Booth was frantic. He and a small group of conspirators had hatched a plan to kidnap Lincoln and take him 100 miles to Confederate authorities in Richmond. This could result in renewed exchanges of prisoners of war or, even better, a negotiated settlement in favor of the Confederate States of America. Booth believed that either way, as ringleader he would be recognized as the savior of the Confederacy.

But in the spring of 1865, as the moment arrived for the kidnapping to unfold, Richmond fell to Union forces and Booth changed the plan: He ordered simultaneous assassinations of President Lincoln, Vice President Andrew Johnson and Secretary of State William Seward. He was convinced the murders would spark so much confusion and turmoil in Washington that the U.S. Congress would sue for peace and the Confederacy would survive. Of course, Booth believed he was born to play the leading role in this final act of the war. So he, personally, would kill the Yankee tyrant.

What follows is a story of Confederate spies and conspirators who were desperate to change the course of the war. It's about their covert dealings before and after Booth fired a bullet into the back of Lincoln's head, leaped down from the President's box onto the dais at Ford's Theater, declared "*Sic semper tyrannis!*" ("Thus always to tyrants!") and exited stage right.

CHAPTER ONE

A Falling Star

OCTOBER 1864

STAGE PRESENCE opened many doors for actor John Wilkes Booth, and on a chilly October day in 1864 he stepped into St. Lawrence Hall hotel in Montreal and registered to stay in Room 150.[1] For the next week, he met with Southern commissioners to Canada and other agents of the Confederate States of America's Department of the North—a fancy name for a mostly autonomous cadre of the Rebel secret service.

Confederate spies were actors, too. Booth's kind of people. From the security of Canada, they were trying to organize Northern and Western sympathizers—generally called Copperheads—in a secret mission to replenish Confederate Gen. Robert E. Lee's battered Army of Northern Virginia in defense of Richmond. A series of covert operations ostensibly would be in retaliation for Union atrocities committed in the South. More important, it would save the Southern capital and the depleted Confederacy.

The plan centered on coordinated jailbreaks to free thousands of Confederate prisoners of war held in northern Ohio and southern New York State. Repatriation of so many seasoned fighting men would rejuvenate Lee's army and reverse what appeared to be certain Southern defeat.

"Your suggestion for a raid upon accessible towns in Vermont, commencing with St. Albans, is approved, and you are required to act in conformity with that suggestion."[2] These are the words of Confederate Commissioner Clement C. Clay, a former U.S. and Confederate senator from Alabama stationed in Montreal. He issued the order under his real name to Confederate cavalry Lt. Bennett Young. Clay typically rearranged letters and signed such correspondence as "T.E. Lacy."[3]

Code names were common for clandestine warriors operating in neutral nations, and, officially, Clay was an authorized liaison officer assigned to work with the Canadian government. Plausible deniability regarding covert actions was important for Clay and his colleagues. But since this order came directly from Confederate authorities in Richmond, he decided its authority must be absolutely clear.

A small Rebel force had already assembled in Canada and the men were eager to fight, but experienced leaders were needed. Confederate agent George N. Sanders and Lt. Young set themselves to the task. Young was one of approximately 120 Confederate soldiers who had escaped from Union prisoners of war camps and lived in Canada. Most of them were of little use in the Southern cause, being removed from battle and no longer taxing federal prison resources. But this mission would be different—an authorized Confederate surprise attack and legitimate act of war deep inside enemy territory.

Lt. Young had previously sailed south from Halifax, Nova Scotia and slipped through the Union blockade into Richmond, where he met with Confederate authorities. They approved the concept for raids originating in Canada against non-traditional targets in the states of Vermont and New York. Young was promoted to first lieutenant and ordered back to Canada to lead the missions.

Jacob Thompson was a U.S. congressman representing Mississippi and had served as the U.S. Secretary of the Interior prior to the outbreak of the Civil War. In 1864, Confederate President Jefferson Davis appointed him as one of the two Confederate commissioners to Canada, where he was stationed in Toronto. Thompson was not sold on the raids because he considered them dishonorable, even though his house and hometown had been torched by U.S. troops.[4] But since he shared authority in Canada with Commissioner Clay, he did not stand in the way of retribution.

Commissioner Clay, agent George Sanders, Lt. Young and others worked directly with the raiders—named the 5th Confederate States Retributers[5]—a 21-man cavalry unit assigned to wreak havoc on citizens in St. Albans, Vermont, as well as those in Buffalo and Rochester, New York, and steal hundreds of thousands of U.S. dollars in the process. If successful, not only would they strike fear deep within enemy territory, they would also rob Yankee banks in all three towns. The proceeds would arm a much larger fighting force to free thousands of imprisoned Rebels in Ohio and New York State.

Buffalo, Rochester and St. Albans are near the Canadian border, and their banks were full of cash. The cities also had populations large enough to generate an anti-war political backlash in the United States. In October 1864, Confederate politicians were willing to sue for peace with honor while those in the U.S. Congress remained divided on the matter.

On October 6, Commissioner Clay ordered Lt. Young to proceed with the attacks. Four days later, Young and two other raiders crossed the border into St. Albans, registered in a hotel and leaked a cover story: They were Canadians from St. John's on a sporting vacation. It worked, even though Young was from Kentucky and his accent was far from Canadian.

The St. Albans area was known for excellent hunting and fishing and supported a healthy guide industry. Ducks had not yet migrated South and their numbers were at the annual high in northern Vermont. Marshes above St. Albans provided roosts for ducks and other waterfowl. Woodcock had not yet left for Southern bottomland forests either. Hunting for ducks, woodcock and ruffed grouse was at its prime. Also, fishing was exceptional for brook trout, pickerel, yellow perch and striped bass. Men reconnoitering routes in and out of St. Albans and asking to buy horses appeared to be preparing for outdoor excursions. Visiting sportsmen were expected in St. Albans. Armed Rebels were not.

Other raiders arrived in St. Albans in twos and threes without attracting notice. All 21 of them were in town in little more than a week. Young began the attack on October 19, leading the troop of Rebel-yelling, pistol-firing raiders on a wild ride down Main Street. They herded residents onto the town commons where Young announced that St. Albans was in possession of the Confederate States of America. Meanwhile, Rebel squads had slipped into the town's three banks and, as one raider engaged a teller about the price of gold, another pulled out a Colt pistol, cocked it and stuck the barrel under the banker's nose.[6]

The robberies in the first city were to be followed by another series in the next city until there was enough money to organize and arm a force large enough to pull off the massive prison breaks needed to re-enforce Lee's army.[7] But subsequent raids never happened.

The St. Albans raiders stole more than $200,000 that day, and most were pleased to have participated in a retaliation for assaults by Union troops on in Southern towns.[8] Darien, Ga., was reduced to charred ruins a year earlier, and it was not the last such atrocity at Yankee hands. However, the assault on unarmed citizens of Darien was not officially sanctioned by U.S. authorities in Washington, and military officers on both sides generally exercised restraint on such activities.

But this year, Union troops had laid to waste to farms in Virginia's Shenandoah Valley, and the destruction of the Confederacy's "breadbasket" smoldered in the minds of the raiders who ran roughshod through St. Albans. Adding to the mood for retribution, residents of occupied Southern cities and those in border states were living under martial law, and many were denied liberty without charges or civilian trials. Elsewhere, Southern citizens whose homes were in contested regions especially suffered. Their belongings were plundered and their houses burned. Revenge was sure to follow.

The St. Albans raid was designed to put Northern citizens and their congressmen on notice: There was a severe price to pay for federal atrocities. More critical to the Southern cause, President Lincoln was running for a second term that November. Such turmoil deep in Yankee territory could inspire a growing, face-saving peace movement in support of the Confederate cause.

It wasn't always that way. On the eve of the Battle of Gettysburg, June 30, 1863, Confederate Gen. Jubal A. Early addressed the people of York, Pennsylvania:

"I have abstained from burning the railroad buildings and car shops in your town because, after examination, I am satisfied the safety of the town would be endangered; and acting in the spirit of humanity, which has ever characterized my government and its military authorities, I do not desire to involve the innocent in the same punishment with the guilty. Had I applied the torch without regard to consequences, I would have pursued a course that would have been fully vindicated as an act of just retaliation for the many authorized acts of barbarity perpetuated by your own army upon our soil. But we do not war upon women and children, and I trust the treatment you have met with at the hands of my soldiers will open your eyes to the monstrous iniquity of the war waged by your government upon the people of the Confederate States, and that you make efforts to shake off the revolting tyranny under which it is apparent to all you are yourselves groaning.

J. A. Early, Major-General C.S.A.[9]

But by July 30, 1864, attitudes had changed. Gen. Early ordered Chambersburg, Pennsylvania burned in retaliation for destruction of public buildings and private homes in Virginia by troops under the command of U.S. Major Gen. David Hunter.[10]

To that end, the St. Albans raiders employed a weapon that each carried in small bottles. "Greek fire" is a mixture of phosphorous and carbon bisulfide developed by a Cincinnati chemist. It combusts upon exposure to oxygen. But the raiders failed to use it properly. Inadequate ventilation, like in a closed room, snuffed out the flame. Also, when thrown against wood siding wet from rain, Greek fire did not ignite typical buildings, much less an entire town. All that burned in St. Albans that day was a woodshed.

The attack was well organized on the front end. The raiders initially exercised restraint when dealing with the residents and managed to exaggerate their troop strength. The locals knew only what they saw and heard. Despite threats of blowing the brains out of citizens who didn't follow instructions, none were killed.[11] But the horses were skittish, not used to riders firing pistols overhead. One raider was thrown from his horse, and Lt. Young shot and wounded a local man through his hand and torso. Also, of the estimated

$200,000 stolen from the banks that day, some was dropped during the mayhem, and raiders probably kept some for themselves.

Although, Lt. Young got all his men out of town, there was no cover from a posted rear guard. The raiders apparently assumed they were the only ones who would test Canada's neutrality in the aftermath. That night and early the next morning, they checked into Canadian hotels and boarding houses, but posted no sentries. It did not take long for the pursuers, with unexpected help from Canadian authorities, to round up 14 of 21 raiders.

Canadian cooperation soon stalled in a tangle of judicial red tape, and protracted diplomatic and legal wrangling to have the men extradited to the United States began. Northerners were outraged. The U.S. government officially protested the enemy operation launched from a neutral nation, and ultimately, the St. Albans raid became a hollow Confederate victory.

Raid organizer George Sanders brought to Confederate operations in Canada international experience in ruthlessness. Earlier, he had made a name for himself by referencing 1852 as "this Brutus of years," which offered among other things the power to bring death to tyrants.[12] In 1853, U.S. President Franklin Pierce appointed Sanders as the American consul to London, but he was recalled a year later after failing to get Senate confirmation. That's because he had been overseas long enough to host a dinner for international revolutionaries and participated in controversial discussions about the proposed assassination of Emperor Napoleon III of France.

In Canada in October 1864, Sanders was again a busy man, and St. Albans was not the only covert operation occupying his time. He was assigned and funded to block extradition from Canada of Lt. Young and the raiders to face military tribunals in the United States. Sanders was also in contact with the radical Rebel preacher Dr. Kensey Stewart and the Rev. Stephen Cameron, who was serving as a Confederate chaplain, about another bold scheme.

Dr. Stewart was a notorious nationalistic Southerner and devout Episcopal minister. Two years earlier, while leading a service at St. Paul's church in occupied Alexandria, Virginia, federal authorities ordered him to bless Abraham Lincoln with a prayer—which he ignored. After the service, soldiers seized the minister at gunpoint and marched him to the guardhouse.[13]

Now he was working on a secret operation for which he had gained an audience with Gen. Robert E. Lee. The preacher explained his plan and asked Lee if he thought such a clandestine action was ethical. Lee was not impressed, and never gave an answer. But Stewart but did get the attention of Confederate Secretary of State Judah Benjamin, who ordered Commissioner Thompson to pay Stewart $20,000.[14]

Benjamin also wrote to the Confederate secretary of war that, "The bearer, Chaplain S.F. Cameron, is employed with Mr. Stewart on a secret service (mission), according to an understanding with the President (Jefferson Davis), and the Chaplain will want to pass through our lines on his way to Canada, accompanied by two friends. Will you give him the necessary papers to enable him to pass with his companions, & oblige?"[15,16]

On October 25, Sanders and Stewart checked into St. Lawrence Hall in Montreal.[17] Chaplain Cameron entered Canada by way of Niagara Falls three weeks later.[18] What was Stewart's secret mission? The answer is in a July 7 letter from Thompson to Secretary of State Benjamin a little more than a month after the commissioner reported for duty in Toronto. Thompson wrote:

> *"Here I met with … the Grand (Master) of the secret order in the western states … All they need now is an 'occasion', as they style it, to rise up and assert their rights … The enrolled strength of the order in Illinois is 85,000. In Indiana it is 56,000 and Ohio is 40,000. In Kentucky unknown, represented as large … The plan is this: Instantaneously, a movement will be made at Chicago, Rock Island and Springfield. These places will be seized and held, the prisoners released, armed and mounted: 7,000 at Chicago, 9,000 at Rock Island."*[19]

To understand Stewart's role, this letter should be read in conjunction with Benjamin's instructions to Commissioner Thompson—which was to follow on November 27: "My present purpose is to explain to you that Dr. Stuart (sic) proposes to engage in the same business as that which you have controlled…"[20] In other words, Stewart was also organizing an uprising against the U.S. government by Southern sympathizers in certain Northern and Western states. It is not known how Thompson perceived this message. But the goal was the same: Free Rebels held as prisoners of war wherever possible and return them to the depleted Confederate army.

Commissioners Clay and Thompson had already agreed to coordinate in this effort. In July, Clay had written to Thompson:

> *"Dr. Massay is here, son-in-law of Medary, and will stay until Friday. He is a high priest in the Sons of Liberty, and can be employed most usefully for us. He and W. might traverse Ohio, Indiana and Illinois by the 20th and have all the organizations ready to act in co-operation."*[21,22]

In late September, Thompson and Clay received a letter by dispatch from Confederate agent J.B. Castleman: "There never has been in this country (Indiana and Illinois) such a time for profitable business, and the time must be taken advantage of." At the bottom of his letter he added: "Please deliver this to Messrs. T. (Thompson) and C (Clay)."[23]

After Stewart arrived in Montreal on October 25, he sent word to Benjamin that he thought there should be a single, massive strike to free the prisoners of war instead of conducting small St. Albans-type retribution raids, which he considered little more than distractions. "I also desire to express my conviction that much, very much, can be done from this side if you give me the time and money, and these fruitless raids are stopped. … If Colonel T. (Thompson) has already created so much alarm and annoyance—and I acknowledge it is very great and expensive—how much more can be done by one great success?"[24,25]

Indeed, the Confederate administration in Richmond had hoped to use the strength of the Copperhead movement in Western states to create a new theater of war, and possibly the creation of a third nation. After the war, some historians tried to link Gen. Early's attack on Chambersburg, Pennsylvania, as part of the sought-after Copperhead "occasion," and the possible formation of a Northwestern Confederacy. But Early discredited such talk as fantasy.[26] While the desire was there, the military wherewithal was not.

Yet Chaplain Cameron's notes affirm the belief held by Confederate operatives in Canada that, within some Northern and Western states, members of certain conservative organizations believed the Confederacy's defeat would water down rights of all states—North, South and West—and weaken the U.S. Constitution.[27]

After agent Sanders arrived in Montreal on October 25, he met first with John Wilkes Booth, who had been there for a week conferring with Thompson and a Confederate blockade runner named Patrick Martin. Booth also played cards with former U.S. consul to England, a Virginian and now a Rebel agent, Beverly Tucker.[28] It is remarkable that, apparently, no federal agents monitoring Confederate activity in Montreal took note of Booth's presence among the Confederate elite. Perhaps none of them were theatergoers, or maybe courtroom theatrics regarding extradition of the St. Albans raiders held their undivided attention.

Also that day, Booth's acquaintance John Deveney strolled across the spacious St. Lawrence Hall lobby after checking his mail in the hotel's post office.[29] He was surprised to see Booth and stopped to talk, assuming the actor was in Montreal for a performance. Deveney was there to avoid the U.S. draft. Casualties in the Union's Army of the Potomac that year exceeded 60,000—or one killed or wounded for every Rebel who faced them. This was more than sufficient to encourage lesser patriots such as Deveney to seek refuge in Canada.

"Are you going to play?" he asked Booth.

"No."

Deveney pushed his inquiry. "What are you going to do?"

"I just came here on a visit, a pleasure trip," Booth said.[30]

Sanders was watching Booth and later asked the actor to join him in Dowley's Barroom for a drink and conversation. Booth had much to learn from agent Sanders, including how to employ a cover story. The men shared a certain recklessness, and both were well suited for covert warfare. Booth certainly was not repulsed by Sanders' philosophy: Tyrannicide was more of a duty than a sin.

Two days later, Booth and blockade runner Patrick Martin entered the Montreal branch of the Bank of Ontario where the actor exchanged $300 in gold coins for sterling notes and a receipt. Martin, who had often slipped across the Potomac River from Virginia into Maryland and back, had learned he was being pursued by federal detectives, so he fled to Canada. Still, he agreed to help Booth move the bound-and-gagged U.S. President across the river into Virginia.

So Martin, who was known to and trusted by Rebel agents in Southern Maryland, wrote a letter that introduced Booth to physicians William Queen and Samuel Mudd. Both were members of a group of doctors with Southern sympathies who, while making house calls, passed important information through Maryland to Confederate authorities.

Booth left Canada the next day, and two weeks later he was in Washington, where he opened an account and deposited $1,500 with the banking firm Jay Cooke and Company. Booth's plot to kidnap Lincoln required operating funds. But prior to going to Canada, he had depleted most of his own savings through bad investments, overly generous sharing, free spending on the kidnapping conspiracy and habitual high living. In his mind, he could not separate the last two.

Literature Cited – Chapter One

1. St. Lawrence Hall Register. 1864-65. Unpublished microfilm. James O. Hall Research Center. Maryland-National Capital Park and Planning Commission. File copy.

2. Headley, J. W., Captain C.S.A. 1906. Confederate Operatives in Canada and New York. The Neale Publishing Company.

3. Boutwell, G.S. 1866. Assassination of Lincoln. Report of House of Representatives. No. 104. 41 pp.

4. Skipwith, P.H. 1882. Notes and Queries: Letter to Rev. J. William Jones. Southern Historical Society Papers. Richmond, Virginia. Digitized by Google. 607 pp.

5. Boutwell, G.S. 1866.

6. Benjamin, L.N. 1865. St. Albans Raid; or, Investigation into the Charges Against Lieut. Bennett H. Young and Command, for Acts at St. Albans, Vt., on the 19th October, 1864. 480 pp.

7. Hayden, H.E. 1882. Notes and Queries: How Many Confederate Towns Did the Enemy Burn During the War? Southern Historical Society Papers. Richmond, Virginia. Digitized by Google. 607 pp.

8. Ibid.

9. Early, J.A. General C.S.A. 1882. The History of a Conspiracy That Failed. Southern Historical Society Papers. Richmond, Virginia. Digitized by Google. 607 pp.

10. Ibid.

11. Benjamin, L.N. 1865.

12. Eyal, Y. 2007. The Young American Movement and the Transformation of the Democratic Party. Cambridge University Press. New York, New York. 266 pp.

13. Cheshire, J.B. 1912. A History of the Protestant Episcopal Church in the Confederate States. New York, London, Bombay and Calcutta: Longmans, Green and Co.

14. Cameron, S.F. (presumed author). Date unspecified. Untitled Manuscript, Notes for a "History of the Confederate Secret Service." Unpublished. James O. Hall Research Center. Maryland-National Capital Park and Planning Commission. File copy. 25 pp.

15. Ibid.

16. Benjamin, J.P. 1864. Letter to Hon. James A. Seddon, Secretary of War, National Archives. M-437, Roll-121.

17. St. Lawrence Hall Register. 1864-65.

18. Fisher, G.P. 1867. Trial of John H. Surratt in the Criminal Court for the District of Columbia, Hon. George P. Fisher Presiding. Vol. 1. Testimony of S. F. Cameron. Government Printing Office. Washington D.C. 678 pp.

19. Cameron, S.F. (presumed author). Date unspecified.

20. Ibid.

21. Ibid.

22. Boutwell, G.S. 1866.

23. Ibid.

24. Ibid.

25. Cameron, S.F. (presumed author). Date unspecified.

26. Early, J.A. General C.S.A. 1882.

27. Cameron, S.F. (presumed author). Date unspecified.

28. Poore, B.P., ed. 1865. Conspiracy trial for the murder of the president, and the attempt to overthrow the government by the assassination of its principal officers. Testimony of Hosea B. Carter. J.E. Tilton and Company. Boston, Massachusetts. 1,577 pp.

29. Poore, B.P., ed. 1865. Conspiracy trial for the murder of the president, and the attempt to overthrow the government by the assassination of its principal officers. Testimony of John Deveney. J.E. Tilton and Company. Boston, Massachusetts. 1,577 pp.

30. Ibid.

A handsome and gifted actor, John Wilkes Booth, traveled to Montreal in October 1864 to obtain Confederate Secret Service support for the kidnapping conspiracy targeting Abraham Lincoln. Library of Congress, BIOG file. Reproduction number LC-DIG-ppmsca-19233.

Lt. Bennett Young led the Confederate retribution raid from Canada against St. Albans, Vt. in October 1864. This image is likely but unconfirmed of Lt. Young. Courtesy of American Civil War Museum and the Virginia Museum of History & Culture.

Commissioner Jacob Thompson attempted to organize the strength on the northern copperhead movement to liberate Confederate prisoners of war, possibly forcing an additional theater of operations in the War of the Rebellion. Library of Congress, Brady-Handy Photograph collection. LC-BH82-5261 A.

Commissioner Clement Clay focused his efforts on retribution raids from Canada. Library of Congress. Illus. in JK 1012.M35 1859.

Secretary of State for the Confederacy, Judah Benjamin, obtained limited cooperation from Commissioner Jacob Thompson. Library of Congress. PH – Unattributed, no. 27 from original photo USZC4-12291.

President Jefferson Davis established the Confederate Department of the North for irregular warfare to be based in Canada and taken against the United States. Library of Congress. PH-Brady (M.), no. 2.

CHAPTER TWO

The Making of a Spy

December 1864–January 1865

THIRTY-SIX HOURS is a long time to worry about being watched,[31] especially for a young woman on her first mission as a courier for the Confederate secret service. Mrs. Sarah Antoinette ("Nettie") Slater, who was in her early 20s, had been on a train that long from Washington City to Montreal by way of Vermont. She was nervous. If caught, the U.S. government might hang her. The papers she carried were direct evidence of espionage.

But Mrs. Slater took some comfort in having an escort—James Fowle, a seasoned Confederate spy. Federal detectives worked trains rolling in and out of Canada, and carefully noted passengers—how they acted, what they talked about and what others overheard them saying.

Just before dawn on December 17, 1864, Mrs. Slater and Fowle arrived at Montreal Station and went to St. Lawrence Hall hotel. She checked into her own room, No. 164,[32] as "A. Reynaud" of New York City. Reynaud was her mother's maiden name, which is French.[33] Mrs. Slater looked French, was fluent in the language, and her mother and her sister lived New York. It was a good alias, one that would not elude her under extreme pressure, and it supported her cover story.

In reality, Mrs. Slater was married to a North Carolina farmer, musician and dance instructor now enlisted in the Confederate Army. She was short, thin and exceptionally attractive—having a pretty face, dark hair and dark eyes.[34] She moved with energy and grace.

Agent Fowle registered as "Jas. Foulke," also of New York, and signed for both of them. His handwriting was neat. The "ulke" in "Foulke" closely matched his cursive strokes for "wle" in his real name.[35] This slight change served the same purpose as Mrs. Slater's choice of an alias and was sufficiently similar to cover a foolish mistake.

St. Lawrence Hall was at the northeast corner of Montreal's St. James and St. Frances Xavier streets. The entry was a covered arcade with shops on each side. As Mrs. Slater walked in, she saw a reading room on one side and a barroom on the other. Then she came to a second hall with the hotel's post office, newspaper stand, library, telegraph bureau and barber shop.[36]

After climbing the grand staircase, she entered a large, open reception area. Guests had begun to stir, and knots of them were engaged in conversations. The adjacent dining hall was sufficiently open to allow patrons to talk confidentially. Two dollars per day covered bed, breakfast, lunch, tea and supper. Southerners were regulars; the hotel barroom served mint juleps. Federal undercover agents were there too.

Three days earlier in Montreal, Judge Charles J. Coursol, who presided in extradition proceedings for the St. Albans raiders, announced that he had no jurisdiction in the matter and ordered the prisoners released.[37] A month earlier, he had recessed the proceedings for 30 days. However, the Canadian government, which was under intense diplomatic pressure from Washington, overruled him and another extradition hearing was set for Superior Court. Canadian police and private detectives employed by the U.S. government tried to re-locate and re-arrest the raiders, some of whom had left Montreal and others had gone underground. Five of the 14 were caught again, including Lt. Young.

St. Lawrence Hall was ground zero for covert operations associated with the Confederate States Department of the North, and Commissioner Clay worked from there. But it was not the only place where secret messages were passed between Canada and Richmond. Commissioner Thompson's primary office was in Toronto, and agent/chaplain Stephen Cameron worked from Saint-Liboire near Quebec City. Mrs. Slater's initial visit to Montreal was brief. She left the next day to move secret information elsewhere in Canada.

On December 21 she was back in St. Lawrence Hall, and again signed in with a man presumed to have been Fowle. But they used different aliases this time. The register noted that "N. Slater and Jim Slater" had checked in to the hotel.[38] Mrs. Slater apparently signed for them, and circumstantial evidence supports the assumption that "Jas. Foulke" and "Jim Slater" were James Fowle. The use of aliases by spies staying at St. Lawrence Hall were typically similar but purposefully inconsistent.

Commissioner Clay often changed the order of letters in his last name to create "Lacy" as his alias. Other examples included those used by Booth's fellow conspirators: "Lewis Paine" for Lewis Powell (Paine was the surname of the family with whom Powell lived in Northern Virginia); "George Azworth" and "George Atwood" for George Atzerodt; and "John Harrison" for John Harrison Surratt.

Secrecy was problematic for Thompson almost from the time he arrived in Canada in May 1864 to begin his job as a commissioner. He made careless mistakes common for amateurs, not the least of which was being too boisterous, which made him stand out in a crowd.

"The bane and curse of carrying out anything in this country is the surveillance under which we act. Detectives, or those ready to give them information, stand at every corner,"[39] he later wrote. Thompson could not move about or meet without being observed, and anyone seen meeting with him was surely watched.[40]

Officially, Canada was neutral during the war. Unofficially, most Canadians were sympathetic to the Confederacy. Anti-Northern sentiment was strong among those in the upper economic classes as well as the bourgeoisie. Union agents reported to Washington that nine of 10 Canadians were rank Rebel sympathizers.[41]

Support for the South was also strong within Canada's military. Canadian military officer George T. Denison offered helpful suggestions to Thompson about getting messages past federal detectives. He recommended writing in pencil on silk and sewing the message inside couriers' collars or cuffs. Silk is thin, light and silent when handled. Penciled writings held up better than ink in wet weather and when laundered.[42] But federal agents were also aware of these methods, and there were no guarantees.

Shoe heels were especially suspect. A spy's shoemaker was trusted not to pass on information to U.S. detectives about customers who had asked to have heels hollowed out for hidden messages.[43] The shoemaker also had to do exceptionally good work to fool the authorities. New heels nailed onto worn shoes and boots were dead giveaways.

All the while, federal detectives were getting better at spotting such techniques. Soon after the Thompson-Denison meeting, U.S. agent R.J. Kimball wrote from Toronto to U.S. Secretary of State William Seward:

> *"The following facts have been given to me ... The rebels in this city have a quick and successful communication with Jeff Davis and the authorities in Richmond in the following manner—written on fine silk and ingeniously secreted in the lining of a coat. These messengers wear metal buttons, which upon the inside, dispatches are minutely photographed, not perceptible to the naked eye, but easily read by the aid of a powerful lens. Letters are written but closely interlined with imperceptible ink (as they call it) to which when a certain chemical is applied is easily deciphered. The messenger arrives in Baltimore, receives additional instructions from 'B ______' and proceeds to Washington, where he undergoes a thorough examination, is searched and permitted to pass. He takes a southeasterly direction to 'Port Tobacco' where he is sheltered by widow 'Mrs. ______' and at dead of night crosses in an India rubber boat to south side of Potomac ..."*[44]

All of which made Mrs. Slater's return trip to Richmond from Canada even riskier. She was pretty, and people noticed her. On the other hand, the longer she stayed at St. Lawrence Hall, the more likely detectives would have her under surveillance before arresting her after her train entered the United States.

Mrs. Slater and an escort left Montreal early on January 3, 1865 and traveled safely to New York City, Baltimore and Washington City. From there they rode by land south to Port Tobacco where they blended in with friendly Marylanders before crossing the Potomac River into Virginia. But this time her escort was not James Fowle. Her escort this trip was Confederate chaplain and secret service agent Stephen Cameron.

Earlier on January 2 in Montreal, Cameron had been busy in advance of this mission. He wrote to Commissioner Thompson in Toronto and sent a telegram to another contact telling them he would leave the next day and was available to take messages to Richmond.[45] That night he dined with Dr. Stewart, the preacher whose plan was to organize Confederate sympathizers in the Western states into a fighting force. Cameron's mission to Richmond could be the last chance to elevate Stewart's influence in Canada.

Before he left for Canada in October, Stewart had been overly direct about raising such an army with Gen. Robert E. Lee, who politely ignored him. More recently from Canada, he sent a letter to President Jefferson Davis which said:

> *"... It cannot be our policy to employ wicked men to destroy the persons & property of private citizens by inhumane and cruel acts. I name only one. $100 of public money has been paid to one Hyams, a shoemaker, for services rendered by conveying and causing to be sold in the city of Washington at auction, boxes of smallpox clothing ..."*[46]

Davis was not impressed. Stewart had foolishly sent through enemy lines an unauthorized letter referencing the Confederacy's financial support of a biological attack. Soon afterward, Secretary Judah Benjamin wrote Thompson in Toronto: "The President does not wish any more money advanced to him (Stewart), nor does he desire any enterprise of any kind be undertaken by the Dr."[47]

Cameron, who had not met Mrs. Slater before traveling south with her, worried that she was too attractive and drew too much attention. Once in Port Tobacco, and with some luck, they planned use a small boat to slip directly across the Potomac with no delays. Having not so good luck meant they would have to stay a night or more at Brawner's Hotel. Cameron's journal notes while in Canada said the following:

"January 1. Attended mass and made visits.
2. Dined with the Doctor. Drove to Beaumont and wrote Col. T. and Swagan.
Sent paper to Swagan. Wrote Pollard and received answer. Wrote again.
Fixed (set) week in January with ________"[48]

Cameron did not note who or which week had been fixed. But eight days later, on January 10, he checked in to St. Lawrence Hall along with Mrs. Slater, according to the register.

Confederate spies and useful covert information crossed the Potomac River under the cover of darkness via two routes. Lt. Charles Cawood commanded a Confederate Signal Corps post on the Virginia side of the river on the northern shore of Mathias Point. Richmond had great need for a steady flow of information via newspapers, letters and encrypted messages. Union generals liked to read their names in the newspapers. Northern reporters reliably tracked their movements and, by extension, that of their commands. The printed word frequently was sensational but also confirmed information flowing from Rebel spies and scouts.

Cawood had a boat, and in good weather his men used it to cross the Potomac at least twice per week picking up mail and messages gathered by Confederate agent Thomas Jones. The Confederacy also took advantage of several less-than-loyal postmasters employed by the U.S. Postal Department in southern Maryland. Jones knew and used them. He also knew and used Dr. Mudd and the physicians' line for collecting and delivering important communications. It took a passenger of unusual importance, high trust and excellent contacts to access the Jones-Cawood route into Virginia.[49]

It's interesting to note that, while Jones was careful, he was not unobserved. Former slave Henry Woodlawn, a free man since November 1, 1864, when the Maryland legislature adopted a new constitution that prohibited slavery, saw signal lights on the Virginia side and a responding answer by Jones. These were followed by a boat he saw coming from Virginia and returning the same night. Woodlawn fished these waters regularly, knew the creeks and the comings and goings on them. This particular boat always started from Virginia. But being observed by Woodlawn did not pose a serious problem for Jones. Woodlawn was Jones' former slave, [50,51] and he remained loyal to his former master—even to the point of lying to federal authorities if need be.

The sharp bend in the river around Mathias Point favored crossers who were evading Union gunboats. Others who ran the blockade, spies included, took a longer route in a more southerly direction across the Potomac, arrived in a creek on the downstream side of Mathias Point, then rowed up a tributary to another Confederate Signal Corps camp operated by Sgt. Harry Brogden.

Brogden's camp was 300 yards uphill from Bridge Creek and five miles upstream from where it entered into the Potomac. Brogden also had a boat, which was stored another half-mile up Bridge Creek. Travelers using his post were required to have a passport signed by the War Department in Richmond. Although the passport system was not absent fraud and had its own black market, it worked well for limited traffic.

Lt. Henry Bascom Smith of the U.S. military intelligence apparatus later noted that one of the best tests of probabilities of whether a person was a deserter or a refugee was the route of travel: "No real deserter or refugee came by way of Harry Brogden's station on the Potomac."[52]

Brogden's rowboat—known as a James River *bateaux*—was almost 26 feet long and could carry up to 16 people counting the crew. Payload was a little more than a ton. It was typically manned by four oarsmen and one steersman. Having less crew, while functional, was significantly slower.

The boat had a flat bottom and shallow draft, enabling navigation through river shoals while heavily loaded. More important, the length and width made it seaworthy enough to row almost two miles across this reach of the Potomac. Its low profile and lead-gray color blended against a backdrop of open water, made it difficult to spot at a distance, even during full daylight. At night the oars were wrapped with rope, especially where the wood rubbed the locks, to muffle the noise. For rare daylight crossings, experienced watermen removed the ropes, which contrasted in color when combined with movement of the oars.[53]

Other tricks were used by blockade runners. Author Thomas Jones, writing 30 years later, noted "that a little before sunset, the reflection of the high bluffs near Pope's Creek extended out into the Potomac till it nearly met the shadows cast by Virginia's woods, and therefore at that time of evening, it was very difficult to observe as small an object floating in the river as a rowboat."[54]

The boats usually left from Virginia before sunset to pick up mail and/or people running the blockade. Given favorable winds and tides, 30 minutes of hard rowing would get them to the Maryland shore. When it was not safe to cross because of federal activity on the Washington side, nearby resident Mary Watson would hang a black cloth over her high dormer window. For crossings after dark, she lit signal lamps from the high windows to broadcast risk levels.

On the Virginia side at that time, Southerners got some lofty help from the national bird of the United States. A bald eagle pair nested each winter in the high pines of Mathias Point. From observation perches near the nest tree and with eyesight second to none in nature, the eagles could see for miles up and down the river. This pair—said to have low regard for noisy Yankee gunboats—flew and cried above the steamers if they got too close. The eagles' trill served as a warning not to put across.[55]

Mrs. Slater and Cameron crossed the Potomac almost immediately after arriving there on January 5 by way of Sgt. Brogden's station. Others were not so fortunate or skilled. Eddy Martin (not to be confused with the elite blockade runner Patrick Martin), was not so lucky, having pre-paid Booth's fellow conspirator George Atzerodt to get him across. For 10 days he was stranded on the Maryland side.[56] Atzerodt offered him only excuses, along with some tidbits about the Lincoln conspiracy, which came out later during the assassination trial.

Literature Cited – Chapter Two

31. Pitman, ed. 1865. The Assassination of President Lincoln and the Trial of the Conspirators. Testimony of Richard Montgomery. Moore, Wilstach & Baldwin. Cincinnati, Ohio. 438 pp.

32. St. Lawrence Hall Register. 1864-65. Unpublished microfilm. James O. Hall Research Center. Maryland-National Capital Park and Planning Commission. File copy.

33. Stanton, J.F. 2011. A Mystery No Longer: The Lady in the Veil. Surratt Courier. A Publication of the Surratt Society & The Maryland-National Capitol Park & Planning Commission.

34. Chaconas, J.L. 1988. Confession of George A. Atzerodt, Published in Baltimore American on January 18, 1869. Surratt Courier. A Publication of the Surratt Society & the Maryland-National Capitol Park & Planning Commission.

35. St. Lawrence Hall Register. 1864-65.

36. Levin, A.L. 1987. "This Awful Drama." Vantage Press, Inc. New York, New York. 248 pp.

37. Benjamin, L.N. 1865. (compiled) The Saint Albans Raid; or Investigation into the Charges Against Lieut. Bennett H. Young and Command for Their Acts at Saint Albans on 19 October 1864. John Lovell. Montreal, Canada. 480 pp.

38. St. Lawrence Hall Register. 1864-65.

39. Cameron, S.F. (presumed author). Date unspecified. Untitled Manuscript, Notes for a "History of the Confederate Secret Service." Unpublished. James O. Hall Research Center. Maryland-National Capital Park and Planning Commission. File copy. 25 pp.

40. Poore, B.P., ed. 1865. Conspiracy trial for the murder of the president, and the attempt to overthrow the government by the assassination of its principal officers. Testimony of Hosea B. Carter. J.E. Tilton and Company. Boston, Massachusetts. 1,577 pp.

41. Kimball, J.R. 1865. Untitled, Letter to Secretary of State William Seward. National Archives. LAS file. M-599, Reel 4.

42. Denison, G.T. Lt. Colonel. 1901. Soldiering in Canada. George N. Morang and Company. 394 pp.

43. Jones, T.A. 1893. J. Wilkes Booth, An Account of His Sojourn in Southern Maryland, after the Assassination of Abraham Lincoln, his Passage Across the Potomac, and his Death in Virginia. Laird & Lee, Publishers. Chicago, Illinois. 126 pp.

44. Kimball, J.R. 1865.

45. Cameron, S.F. (presumed author). Date unspecified.

46. Boutwell, G.S. 1866. Assassination of Lincoln. Report of House of Representatives. No. 104. 41 pp.

47. Cameron, S.F. (presumed author). Date unspecified.

48. Ibid.

49. Jones, T.A. 1893.

50. Oldroyd, O.H. 1901. The Assassination of Abraham Lincoln. Privately printed. Washington D.C. 167 pp.

51. Woodlawn, H. 1865. Unpublished Statement to Detectives Given April 30, 1865. National Archives. LAS file. M-599, Reel 6.

52. Smith, H.B. 1915. Between the Lines Secret Service Stories Told Fifty Years After. Booz Brothers. New York, New York. 343 pp.

53. Jones, T.A. 1893.

54. Ibid.

55. Conrad, T.N., Captain C.S.A. 1892. A Confederate Spy. J. S. Ogilvie Publisher. New York, New York. Digitized by Google. 142 pp.

56. Fisher, G.P. Hon. Presiding. 1867. Trial of John H. Surratt in the Criminal Court for the District of Columbia. Washington Government Printing Office. Testimony of Eddy Martin. 678 pp.

CHAPTER THREE

Richmond and Back

JANUARY 1–11, 1865

ABSENT FOR THREE WEEKS, Mrs. Slater safely returned to Richmond on January 6, 1865, and saw little had changed in the besieged Confederate capital. Food and supplies continued to be scarce—tea cost $100 per pound and wood $100 per cord—yet most residents understood the situation and dealt with the inconveniences. What they didn't know was the Confederate national debt had exceeded $300 million, and the government was paying $1 in gold for $60 of its own paper money.[57]

"There is a deep vexation in the city—a general apprehension that our affairs are rapidly approaching a crisis such as has not been experienced before," Confederate war clerk J.B. Jones noted in his diary. Even so, "Rich men are generally indignant … (they) have not yet awakened to a consciousness that there is a danger of losing all …"[58]

Abraham Lincoln had been re-elected president, and the United States' resolve to win the war was absolute. With his second inauguration only two months away, time was running out for the South. Atlanta had fallen and Confederate war supplies no longer moved through that city's railroad terminus and distribution hub. Confederate Gen. John Bell Hood's battered troops had retreated to Tennessee, and the Shenandoah Valley—once the "Breadbasket of the Confederacy"—had been laid to waste and lost.

Gen. Robert E. Lee and his Army of Northern Virginia were dug in at Petersburg, Virginia, between Richmond and the Union Army, now commanded by Gen. U.S. Grant. Neither side had significant success in the trenches since the previous summer when Pennsylvania coal miners-turned-soldiers tunneled under Lee's line and blasted what became known as "the Crater." Confederate troops in Mahone's Division closed the break, turning initial Union success into a costly, highly publicized disaster. In the counterattack, the 61st Virginia captured multiple colors along with Union Gen. William Francis Bartlett.[59,60] The Crater would long be remembered by the federals as "the horrid pit."

Gen. Grant knew he could win a war of attrition right there from the trenches, and Gen. Lee knew he could not win with his ragged army immobilized and near starvation. So Lee and Confederate president Davis decided to make a bold move. Confederates had ammunition and stores that could support a major campaign.[61] But first Lee had to move his army, and the timing of the withdrawal would have to balance military objectives with public and political perceptions. Lee and Davis were aware of the high risks, yet remained optimistic.

Meanwhile, the Confederate government in Richmond, specifically the War Department, was wracked by turmoil. The origin of their woes was self-inflicted. On the second morning of the new year, a frail Secretary of War, James Alexander Seddon, sat with his gray head between his knees[62] and wondered how much longer he could do his job. He and Davis were at odds, as were members of the Confederate Congress. Most of the problems were born of corruption.

Early in his tenure, Seddon extended favors by providing passports across lines into the North and back, a situation exacerbated by Baltimore's "Plug Uglies," a violent, political street gang displaced to Richmond by the imposition of martial law in Maryland. Some of these men worked civilian law enforcement in Richmond and got hold of a significant quantity of passports. Black market sale of passports was a Yankee spy's dream for getting in and out of Richmond undetected. An official complaint was lodged with Seddon's department by Confederate Col. D.J. Godwin regarding what seemed to be a never-ending flow of troublesome interlopers.

Seddon had also granted numerous conscription exemptions, including one for the son of Confederate Congressman Jackson Morton of Florida. Young Morton had made his way—"escaped," as it was termed—from Washington to Richmond and his exemption from military service was issued one day after others in similar circumstances were conscripted into the Army of Northern Virginia.[63]

Adding to the scandal, Lee's troops, facing an entire winter in Petersburg, had only a few days rations left, and Seddon, who directed a committee in charge of providing food for to them, was accused of hiding barrels of wheat flour on his property and getting top dollar for any sold to the Confederate government. He received $40 per barrel while impressed flour from other farms brought barely $10.[64] Those lacking political connections had no choice but to sell.

Also at that time, War Department clerk Jones wrote in his diary that a lack of nutrition had stolen his health as well that of his family. He wanted to fish for food, he wrote, but could not find suitable hooks in Richmond. He noted that he could buy only a little wheat while Seddon's personal clerk received wheat flour in abundance.[65] Cronyism and corruption were ruining morale, he wrote.

Meanwhile, in the midst of all this turmoil, pretty spy Nettie Slater had thoroughly impressed her handlers in the Confederate State Department. In her first covert mission, she carried dispatches north of the Potomac River, across the border between Canada and the United States, moved messages within Canada, and returned with dispatches from Confederate authorities in Canada to Richmond. She accomplished all of this during heightened activity by the U.S. detectives working to halt Rebel communications about the trial of the St. Albans raiders. The detectives had a good understanding of techniques used in and around the Confederacy's Canadian operations, yet Mrs. Slater slipped through their net. Grueling travel conditions and prolonged exposure to winter weather failed to deter her.

Stephen Cameron's work was also impressive. He had left Canada with

Mrs. Slater early on January 3 and arrived in Richmond on January 6,[66] and both were ordered to immediately return to Canada and take only four days in the process, circumstances permitting. Secretary of State Benjamin had an urgent letter and other correspondence that needed to be delivered to Commissioner Thompson about new leadership assigned to the Confederate Department of the North.

Getting to Canada in four days was a huge challenge. Previously, in a letter to U.S. Secretary of State Seward, detective J. R. Kimball wrote that a round-trip spy mission from Richmond to Montreal required 14 days.[67] Mrs. Slater and Cameron were about to prove him wrong.

Late on January 6, they took a train from Richmond to Milford, Virginia, two miles southwest of Bowling Green, where they hired a carriage to Port Royal, a distance of almost 16 miles. They crossed the Rappahannock River by ferry and rode overland 20 miles to Sgt. Brogden's Signal Corps station and waited until sunset to cross the Potomac into southern Maryland, then went overland to Washington City for the 36-hour train ride to Montreal.[68]

Cameron—whose alias was T.F. Hendrickson—and Mrs. Slater stepped off the train into the bitter cold of Montreal late on January 10. They checked into Rooms 181 and 182 at St. Lawrence Hall, noting they were from Connecticut, which was Mrs. Slater's home state prior to moving to North Carolina.[69] The next day Cameron wrote in his journal: "Dispatched letter to Mrs. T January 11." "Mrs. T" was code for Commissioner Thompson. The letter was from Secretary Benjamin and dated December 30, 1864:

> *Dear Sir,*
> *I send you by present conveyance duplicate of papers forwarded about a week ago and copies of some former letters. On the 6th inst. I wrote you by private hand a letter from which the following is an extract:*
>
> *The political objectives contemplated at the time of your departure from Richmond being at an end, the President supposes you may desire to return home, etc.*
>
> *I have now to inform you that from reports which reached us from trustworthy sources we are satisfied that so close espionage is kept upon you that your services have been deprived of the value which is attached to your*

further residence in Canada. The President thinks, therefore, that as soon as the gentleman arrives who bears this letter of which I have given you an extract above, it will be better that you transfer to him as quietly as possible all of the information that you have obtained and the release of funds in your hands and then return to the Confederacy.

Hoping soon to see you and to obtain from you in person a full account of all that has occurred since we parted, I have the honor to remain …
Very respectfully,

Yr. obdt. st.
J.P. Benjamin
Secretary of State"[70]

Proof beyond doubt of the identity of "T.F. Hendrickson" was never determined, and neither was confirmation of the mission from Canada to Richmond and back January 3-10. But a preponderance of circumstantial evidence is solid.

On December 28, Cameron checked into Room 148 at St. Lawrence Hall.[71] On December 30, he received a letter from "Col. T" and wrote a response. He made journal entries on December 30, January 1 and January 2—thus confirming he was in Canada on those days.[72] But afterwards, there were eight days absent of journal entries or other records of his whereabouts. Eight days is how long a round-trip mission to Richmond with no layover could be made, and Cameron was experienced enough to do so. He would not carry a journal while traveling covertly because if caught, his career in espionage would end—as would his life in all likelihood.

Two and a half days was as fast as spies could move between Washington and Richmond in 1865. This was later documented when John Surratt and Mrs. Slater made it to Washington during the fall of Richmond. And in May 1863, a Rebel spy named Thomas Conrad made the trip from Northern Virginia to Washington in three days.[73] The addition of 36-38 hours aboard trains between Washington and Montreal,[74] and a one-way trip from Richmond to Montreal would equal four days.

On January 11, the day after Mrs. Slater and Cameron checked in at St.

Lawrence Hall, Cameron's journal entries noted that he had dispatched a letter to Thompson. In other words, he did not write a letter, he delivered one. Also, a copy of the December 30 letter from Secretary Benjamin to Thompson was included in Cameron's post war, untitled manuscript about his Confederate secret service.

Throughout the manuscript, Cameron included key correspondences, presumably those that he had surreptitiously carried. No other dispatches that compete with these critical dates in late 1864 and early 1865 are included. Thus, the evidence strongly indicates that Cameron carried the notice, or a duplicate copy, from Secretary Benjamin that relieved Commissioner Thompson of his post in Canada.[75]

All told, Steven Cameron had registered at St. Lawrence Hall using his true name three times in December 1864,[76] but switched to his alias, "T.F. Hendrickson," on January 11, 1865. Why? He was a married Episcopal minister, which would not have gone over well if it got out that he had checked into a hotel escorting a beautiful young lady who wasn't his wife. "T.F. Hendrickson" appeared on the St. Lawrence Hall register twice in 12 months from mid-1864 through mid-1865, and both times he had escorted a beautiful young woman who turned out to be Mrs. Slater.[77]

"T.F. Hendrickson" does not show up elsewhere in any Civil War records. But timing and location of known activities by Stephen Cameron coincident with the arrival of "Mr. Hendrickson" were telling in January 1865. It came up again that April when Lincoln conspirator John Surratt was on the run following the president's assassination. Two Confederate spies connected with Surratt were in New York State or possibly Vermont, and helped him slip into to Canada, where he could lay low. "T.F. Hendrickson" was one of the spies and Mrs. Slater was the other.

Previously, on January 10, 1865, newly commissioned Confederate Gen. Edwin Gray Lee—a cousin of Gen. Robert E. Lee—and his wife boarded a train in Halifax on the first leg of a long trip across eastern Canada to Montreal. One month prior to that, they left Fort Fisher on the North Carolina coast and ran the Yankee blockade into Nova Scotia. To disguise the purpose of his new Canada assignment, Lee carried doctor's orders furloughing him to recuperate in a cold climate from tuberculosis. It was an interesting cover;

he in fact had tuberculosis. If cold temperatures could improve the health of his lungs, 30-below-zero certainly fit the bill.

The Lees traveled by sleigh across the iced-over St. Lawrence River and eastern Canada. In his possession, but carefully concealed, was a letter written by Secretary Benjamins to Commissioner Thompson that said in part, "The political objectives contemplated at the time of your departure from Richmond being at an end, the President supposes you may desire to return home..."[78] Edwin Gary Lee was assigned to be Thompson's replacement.

Meanwhile, St. Albans raider Lt. Young was ready to testify in his extradition case in Montreal, and he was worried—an apprehension not absent justification. Hanging and extradition were synonyms to the raiders, and Lt. Young was well aware of the fact that Union authorities would waste no time executing him after arriving in the United States.

Confederate agent Lt. S.B. Davis had arrived in Montreal a week previously carrying paperwork from Richmond documenting that the raiders were soldiers, not civilian outlaws. He volunteered to return to Richmond and retrieve more documentation but was arrested in route by federal detectives, and within three days of his capture was sentenced to hang as a spy.[79] With that, however, the U.S. government failed to impress Canada's Superior Court about the likelihood of a fair trial and justice in the case against the raiders if extradited.

Lt. Bennett Young went before Canadian Judge Smith and testified convincingly that extradition would be a death sentence.[80] On January 11, Smith recessed the hearing, and the raiders got 30 days more to prove they were soldiers and not civilian outlaws when they terrorized and robbed the citizens of St. Albans.[81]

Literature Cited – Chapter Three

57. Jones, J.B. 1866. A Rebel War Clerk's Diary. J.B. Lippincott & Co. Philadelphia, Pennsylvania. 482 pp.

58. Ibid.

59. Bussler, M. (director). 2010. Shot to Pieces. Docudrama of Harvard Student William F. Bartlett.

60. Trask, B.H. 1988. 61st Virginia Infantry. The Virginia Regimental History Series. H. E. Howard, publisher. 120 pp.

61. Jones, J.B. 1866.

62. Ibid.

63. Ibid.

64. Ibid.

65. Ibid.

66. Cameron, S.F. (presumed author). Date unspecified. Untitled manuscript, notes for a "History of the Confederate Secret Service." Unpublished. James O. Hall Research Center. Maryland-National Capital Park and Planning Commission. File copy. 25 pp.

67. Kimball, J.R. 1865. Untitled, Letter to Secretary of State William Seward. National Archives. LAS file. M-599, Reel 4.

68. Smith, H.B. 1915. Between the Lines Secret Service Stories Told Fifty Years After. Booz Brothers. New York, New York. 343 pp.

69. St. Lawrence Hall Register. 1864-65. Unpublished microfilm. James O. Hall Research Center. Maryland-National Capital Park and Planning Commission. File copy.

70. Cameron, S.F. (presumed author). Date unspecified.

71. St. Lawrence Hall Register. 1864-65.

72. Cameron, S.F. (presumed author). Date unspecified.

73. Conrad, T., Captain C.S.A. 1904. The Rebel Scout. The National Publishing Company. Washington City. 232 pp.

74. Hall, J.O. 1990. Unpublished letter to Dr. Alford. James O. Hall Research Center. Maryland-National Capital Park and Planning Commission. File copy.

75. Cameron, S.F. (presumed author). Date unspecified.

76. St. Lawrence Hall Register. 1864-65.

77. Ibid.

78. Cameron, S. F. (presumed author). Date unspecified.

79. Benjamin, L.N. 1865. (compiled). The Saint Alban's Raid; or Investigation into the Charges Against Lieut. Bennett H. Young and Command for Their Acts at Saint Alban's on 19 October 1864. John Lovell. Montreal, Canada. 480 pp.

80. Ibid.

81. Ibid.

CHAPTER FOUR

The Conspirators

January 1–21, 1865

JOHN WILKES BOOTH registered in Washington's National Hotel on New Year's Eve 1864 and stayed a week and a half.[82] While there, he enlisted the help of John Harrison Surratt in the plan to abduct President Lincoln. Since last November, Surratt had been living at his mother's boarding house at 541 H. Street, several blocks east of the White House.

Surratt's help was not easily earned. Booth showed Surratt the letter of introduction he had secured from Confederate agents during his October trip to Canada, and he met with him several times. "It's useless for you, Mr. Booth, to seek any information from me at all," Surratt had insisted before asking, "What are your intentions?" Booth leaned close to Surratt and whispered, "It's to kidnap President Lincoln and carry him off to Richmond."[83]

Later, after careful consideration, Surratt told Booth he would join the conspiracy. If Lincoln was taken as a prisoner of war, surely the U.S. government would resume exchanges—greatly relieving manpower-starved Confederate fighting forces as well as the cost of operating overcrowded camps packed with captured Union soldiers. The exchange rate for the President would be huge—one Yankee general had previously fetched 46 privates.

Much like Booth, Surratt was a daring Southern sympathizer and a bit of a dandy. The tall, slender 20-year-old was streetwise and confident and disdained federal agents, later saying he had never been around more stupid detectives than those employed by the U.S. government. "They seemed to have no idea whatever on how to search men."[84]

His earlier service to the cause included work as a disloyal U.S. postmaster, after getting the job vacated at the death of his hard-drinking father in 1862. Envelopes mailed inside other envelopes were effective in getting useful information, including newspapers, into sympathetic hands, which passed them on to authorities in Richmond who tracked the whereabouts of Union generals and their troops. In addition, coded classified newspaper ads provided them with surreptitious messages from undercover agents. But Surratt eventually came under suspicion and lost his post office job.

Next he was employed as a Confederate courier, moving information between Washington and Richmond. Starting in the summer of 1864, he expanded his reach to Canada and back. He was also well connected to members of the secretive Confederate Signal Corps, Dr. Samuel Mudd and the network of spying physicians, Rebel agents in Baltimore and other operatives.

Booth's general list of conspirators included Mudd, who had previously assisted him with logistics in southern Maryland. Mudd provided an escort for Booth to meet with a trusted blacksmith in Port Tobacco. This led to the actor's purchase of a horse he planned to use in Lincoln's abduction. Mudd also arranged for Booth's lodging in the southern Maryland countryside while he schemed and reconnoitered there. Mudd introduced Booth to other contacts, including Thomas Harbin, who served in the Confederate Signal Corps and had connections in Richmond all the way up to Jefferson Davis. Booth planned to use Harbin to help bundle Lincoln out of Maryland and across the Potomac River into Virginia.[85] He could also assist in determining when and where Lincoln was most vulnerable for capture.

Surratt had ties to Harbin already, but Booth asked Mudd to introduce him to his new co-conspirator. The doctor did not know that Surratt and Booth had met previously. This was Booth's way of compromising Mudd and assuring his continued cooperation as well as silence.

Louis Weichmann, a clerk in the U.S. War Department, was a friend of John Surratt and a resident at Mary Surratt's boarding house. John Surratt used him to obtain useful information. Weichmann's job with the federal government included administrative support for prisoner-of-war exchanges. He even took Surratt on a tour of the War Department where he introduced him to coworkers. But Weichmann could neither ride a horse nor shoot a pistol, thus was not included on the team of kidnappers.[86]

In a span of three months, Booth and Surratt compromised Mudd, the slow-witted boatman George Atzerodt, Weichmann, a friend named Sam Arnold and actors John Matthews and Samuel Knapp Chester. Most of them would later pay high prices for their alliances.

The conspirators' greatest challenge at that time was to catch and subdue Lincoln, an experienced wrestler, then slip across the Potomac River into Virginia before chaos yielded to coordination in the federal response. Thomas Jones, who ran a covert Confederate Signal Corps operation on the Maryland side of the river, later authored a book about Lincoln's assassination that included details about the kidnap plot. Lincoln was to be subdued with chloroform, gagged and placed in a carriage, driven south through Maryland to the Potomac River and into Virginia.

Another challenge would be getting the carriage and Lincoln over the well-guarded south bridge out of Washington. The kidnappers agreed to shoot the sentries if necessary, knowing they would have fresh horses waiting along the route and that whoever was chasing them would not know their destination.[87,88]

Word had gotten out about some details of the operation but not enough to spoil the plan. Confederate Signal Corps operator Jones was not a part of the kidnapping network but got wind of the plan. Also, local waterman Richard Smoot had heard about the relays of fresh horses.[89]

When they reached the Potomac, the kidnappers planned to put Lincoln in a boat and row almost two miles across the river before federal gunboat captains could organize a search.[90] Once on the Virginia side, Signal Corps courier Benjamin B. Arnold would take Lincoln to his house overlooking the Potomac and hold him there for the arrival of Confederate Lt. Col. John Singleton Mosby's cavalry, which would whisk the President south to

Richmond.[91] It was a role that Mosby—known as the infamous Grey Ghost—did not know about at that time.

While the kidnapping plans were being laid, Weichmann noticed that Surratt had enough spending money to come and go as he pleased,[92] even though he had a reputation of being unemployed, broke and in debt. Also, Weichmann was present when Dr. Mudd introduced Booth to Surratt. But Weichmann knew nothing of Surratt working as a paid Confederate courier at that time.

Years later, Surratt tried to make money from self-aggrandizing lectures about his role in the Lincoln conspiracy. He claimed that Confederate Secretary of State Judah Benjamin "gave me the dispatches and $200 in gold with which to pay my way to Canada. That was the only money I ever received from the Confederate government or any of its agents."[93]

However, Confederate secret service chief Edwin Gray Lee documented a payment to Surratt for reconnoitering the Union's prison camp at Elmira, New York, as well as multiple payments to him after the assassination while Surratt was hiding in Canada.[94]

Weichmann was one of a half-dozen long-term boarders at Mary Surratt's house. Others came and went regularly. Generally, bed space was made available by doubling up for critical needs. Surratt family acquaintance Thomas Nelson Conrad was also welcomed to stay at any time.

Confederate War Department clerk J.B. Jones noted in his journal that Conrad was a Confederate secret agent.[95] He was well-suited for spying because he avoided attracting attention to himself in Washington. He got money from Richmond to support a network of Southern spies that worked in Washington, and he communicated directly with Confederate Secretary of War James A. Seddon. One of the spies of Conrad's network may have been John Surratt, although this was never confirmed.

On January 10, 1865, Conrad wrote to Seddon:

> *"Our agents write me from Washington for funds. Let me therefore give a statement and ask for an order. I received from the Hon. Secretary of State, Mr. Benjamin, last September, $400 in gold, which yielded me $1,000 in northern funds. This has borne the expenses of five of us for four months,*

> *(including two horses) averaging $50 a month therefor. You at once perceive the economy that we have practiced. It would have been much more had we not used our private funds in many instances. If our services have been satisfactory, I would be obliged if the honorable secretary would, at his pleasure, remit a draft which I can have cashed, I presume, and then relieve us of embarrassment and encourage us to continue our labors. Commending it to your attention, I am.*
>
> *Respectfully, your obedient servant,*
> *Thomas M. Conrad*
>
> *Upon hearing from you, I shall leave for Washington, unless otherwise ordered by you."*[96]

This correspondence was in a report by U.S. Rep. George Boutwell's congressional committee following the Lincoln assassination. But a copy error was made regarding Conrad's name. The middle initial was supposed to be "N" for "Nelson" not "M."

In early January after meeting with Booth, Surratt took leave without permission from his new job with the Adams Express Company and never returned, not even to collect his pay. During that time, he went to Port Tobacco in southern Maryland and asked Atzerodt for help finding a boat to run the blockade. Suitable boats were not readily available. On January 14, Surratt and Harbin bought one from local waterman Smoot for $250, paying half up front. It was a flat-bottomed wooden boat, lead-gray in color,[97] a basic workhorse for Potomac blockade-runners and exactly what would be needed to get the kidnappers and their captive across the river.

Atzerodt was not very bright. He soaked what little cognitive skills he had in regular alcohol baths, and his drinking reinforced another unfortunate trait—he talked too much. He was a German immigrant without a sufficient grasp of English, although what grasp he did have he used excessively. He told Eddy Martin, who had been waiting in Port Tobacco for almost two weeks to put across to Virginia, that he had been busy buying boats.[98] He also talked about relays of fresh horses planned between Washington and Port Tobacco. It is no wonder that word of the planned kidnapping got out. But

Atzerodt knew how to row and how to navigate the Potomac River in the dark, and the conspirators needed him.

While Surratt was in Port Tobacco, Booth worked Baltimore with his first two recruits to the conspiracy: friends from his childhood Samuel Arnold and Michael O'Laughlen. The three of them secured two Spencer repeating rifles, handcuffs, revolvers, rope and other equipment for the kidnapping. Transporting the gear by train to Washington would surely attract attention, so Arnold and O'Laughlen agreed to deliver it themselves at the time and place for their use. Booth returned to his room in Washington's National Hotel on January 12[99] and stayed there for most of the month.

Also in January, a strong, young Southerner rode into a Union camp in northern Virginia, gave his name to authorities as Lewis Paine, took the U.S. Oath of Allegiance, passed through Yankee lines and went to Baltimore. Misses Maggie and Mary Branson were on his mind. But Paine was neither a run-of-the-mill refugee dodging service in the Confederate Army nor a deserter. Had federal officers known his history, they would not have accepted his oath. They would have arrested him as a spy.

"Lewis Paine" was the name he claimed later that year when he left this world with his head in a noose, but it was not what he was given upon his arrival. He was Lewis Powell, a Confederate soldier in a Florida regiment of Gen. A.P. Hill's corps before being wounded and captured in 1863 at Gettysburg. He was put to work as an orderly, aiding wounded Confederate prisoners and met volunteer nurse Maggie Branson, who was in Gettysburg from Baltimore to help wounded Rebels. Miss Branson did not hide her Southern sympathies. As temporary hospitals in and around Gettysburg closed, she returned to Baltimore.

Many of the wounded and captured Confederates were sent to Baltimore for treatment at what was called the West Buildings Hospital, originally a cotton warehouse ill-suited for providing medical care. Powell accompanied them because the federals needed prison nurses. Maggie Branson resumed her volunteer service there, and later assisted in Powell's escape by slipping him a blue uniform, as well as $10 in bribe money she had baked in a cake. Once out, he made his way to Branson's Boarding House, at 16 Elmwood St., where he met Maggie's sister, Mary, before returning to Virginia in September.

By the end of that month, Powell was attached to the 43rd Virginia Battalion obviously with the approval of the commander, Lt. Col. Mosby. For the next year and a quarter, Powell served in Mosby's Partisan Rangers. He was good at it, even inspiring a line of poetry written by an admiring Confederate soldier: "… the terrible Lewis Powell."

By mid-January 1865, Lewis Powell—using the name "Paine"—was back in the company of Mary and Maggie Branson. The Branson spinsters, who were 10 years or more his senior, gave him a room and free reign in their boarding house. The sisters knew Baltimore well, including clandestine operatives working there for Southern independence. One of them—Preston Parr—was introduced to Powell, and questions about his Southern loyalty and credentials were not necessary. Authentication by the sisters was enough for Parr, owner of a Baltimore china shop.

On January 21, one week after Powell took the oath and passed through Union lines, Surratt and Weichmann took a train from Washington to Baltimore[100] and registered in Room 127 of the Maltby House. Surratt went to Baltimore for a meeting with Parr, and, as usual, Weichmann was excluded from discussions about the kidnapping. But he had other business in Baltimore, and remained clueless about being compromised by traveling and rooming with a covert Confederate agent.

Surratt took a carriage to meet with Parr and Lewis Powell at the china shop about the kidnapping plot. With Powell in the mix, the conspiracy got much-needed muscle—a man who served with the Mosby's rangers, the cavalry troop that they planned to use to transport Lincoln from the Virginia side of the Potomac River to Richmond.

It has been generally assumed that Surratt recruited Powell—who was erroneously considered a Confederate deserter—to Booth's team of conspirators. But if he was a deserter, surely Booth and the others would have excluded him from participating in the mission. And why would wily John Surratt abandon caution and take into confidence a stranger, much less a deserter? It's also highly unlikely that Powell, if he was a Rebel deserter, would have joined conspirators who would be working closely with his former cavalry unit.

Mosby's Rangers were called "feather-bed" soldiers by envious Confederate soldiers serving in regular units. Powell and his fellow cavalrymen lived at home or with other families in Northern Virginia. They gathered to get special assignments, completed their assignments and returned to where they lived. Rangers slept comfortably and ate better than line troops, and while Powell was living with the Paine family, he had a Virginia girlfriend just down the road from where he was bivouacked. He would have been a fool to desert Mosby's Rangers.

Powell apparently had volunteered, or possibly was ordered, to take a special assignment—at the time details likely unknown—that would place him into the kidnapping plot. Surely he was not recruited by Booth or Surratt. In a mere seven days, he had entered a Union camp, taken the oath of allegiance to the United States, gone to Baltimore to see the Branson sisters and met Preston Parr. In turn, Parr contacted Surratt, and asked him to come to the china shop to meet Powell. Surratt agreed, and went to Baltimore, where Powell also joined the plot. All of this fell in place in just one week. More than likely Powell was assigned to this duty by Mosby's second in command because the Colonel had been wounded and out of action for six weeks.[101]

Booth was happy to have talked John Surratt into joining him as a co-conspirator if indeed that was the way their conversations really unfolded. With Surratt came access to at least two safe houses: Mrs. Surratt's boarding house in Washington, and Lloyd's tavern—at Surrattsville—also owned by Mary Surratt and leased by the drunkard John Lloyd. Surratt had also teamed up with Lewis Powell and recruited David Herold.

On or around January 14, Surratt purchased a boat and recruited oarsman Atzerodt to row the captive President across the Potomac to Virginia as planned. Herold, who worked in the Navy Yard pharmacy in Washington, could get chloroform on short notice. He was also an avid quail hunter that knew most of the farmers and nearly every back road and deer trail in the two counties south of the city. He could get to numerous Potomac River launching sites in southern Maryland. But most important, Herold was loyal to his heroes: Booth and Surratt. They were leaders; Herold was a follower.

Almost too quickly it seems, John Surratt had become as critical to the plot to kidnap Lincoln as was John Wilkes Booth. All of which begs the following questions regarding their world of lies, half-truths, deceptions and omissions:

- Who recruited John Wilkes Booth?
- How could Booth, an actor, have known the comings and goings of the President of the United States without having reconnoitered the White House?
- Did he just happen to have a kidnapping plan that was a near-perfect match of one developed by covert Confederate agent Thomas N. Conrad, who did reconnoiter the White House?
- How did Booth learn the existence of the secret service work done through the Confederacy's Department of the North?
- How would he know who to contact when he arrived in Montreal?
- And why would any of the Confederate elites trust Booth enough to write a letter of introduction for him and provide him funding?

Answers to these questions may be found in a series of coincidences—so numerous as suggest a trend—involving Thomas Conrad. First, Conrad knew the Surratt family before the onset of war, and took multiple meals at their tavern in Surrattsville during the early years of the conflict.

Later in the war, on August 27, 1864, Conrad was ordered to take leave from his cavalry unit then serving near Shepherdstown, West Virginia to report to Richmond for a special assignment. He then left Richmond for Washington City carrying orders dated September 15, 1864 which directed Col. Mosby (Confederate cavalry) and Lt. Cawood (Confederate Signal Corps—Potomac River crossing) to support him. Upon arrival in Washington, he immediately began monitoring Lincoln's movements and determined to kidnap Lincoln without delay on one of his frequent travels between the White House and Soldier's Home—the Lincoln kidnapping clearly was Conrad's special assignment. Conrad was ready to execute the plan and grab Lincoln when inexplicably the president started traveling with a cavalry escort. Conrad aborted the kidnapping attempt because of Lincoln's new escort, but he did not return to Virginia until November 24, at least seven weeks later.

At the time of Conrad's return to Virginia, John Wilkes Booth was beginning his coordination of logistics with Dr. Samuel Mudd in southern Maryland which in turn would lead Booth to contact John Harrison Surratt. Unless in the obscured and hazy reality, it was Conrad's friend John Surratt who actually reached out and contacted Booth.

Conrad would later write that his duties as a Confederate scout carried him to Canada. He offered no details as to exactly where in Canada, when he was there, or the purpose. Eliminating dates when he was known to be elsewhere leaves early October through the middle of November of 1864 as the only dates possible for him to go there. It is interesting to note that these dates overlap the dates John Wilkes Booth was known to be in Montreal meeting with Confederate elites.

When he wasn't on duty with his regular military unit or in Washington City, Conrad operated from a woods camp, "the eagle nest," on the Virginia bank of the Potomac. The second in command of his four-man scouting unit on the Virginia side was Lt. Mortimer Ruggles. After Lee surrendered at Appomattox, Ruggles riding with Privates Absalom Bainbridge and William Jett—all three riding away from their homes at a time when the entire remainder of the Army of Northern Virginia was returning to their homes defeated—encountered Davy Herold and John Wilkes Booth at the Rappahannock ferry and assisted them to hide with friendly locals during their flight from federal justice following the assassination.

When Booth crossed the Rappahannock River and was guided to the Garrett farm, he was double mounted with Lt. Ruggles on a sorrel that had four white feet and a white front. Booth was riding "Old Whitie," which just happened to be Thomas Nelson Conrad's favorite scouting horse.[102]

History has portrayed Booth as the man who originally planned the Lincoln kidnapping and changed it at the last minute into a presidential assassination. But more than likely, Booth himself was recruited to kidnap Abraham Lincoln in a desperate attempt to turn the tide of war and save the Confederacy.

Literature Cited – Chapter Four

82. Poore, B.P., ed. 1865. Conspiracy trial for the murder of the president, and the attempt to overthrow the government by the assassination of its principal officers. Testimony of G.W. Bunker. J.E. Tilton and Company. Boston, Massachusetts. 1,577 pp.

83. Surratt, J.H. 1870. Lecture at Rockville, Maryland. Transcript carried in December 7, 1870 edition of the Evening Star newspaper, Washington, D.C.

84. Ibid.

85. Chaconas, J.L. 1988. Statement of George A. Atzerodt to Prov. Mar. McPhail in Presence of John L. Smith on the night of May 1, 1865. Surratt Courier. A Publication of the Surratt Society & The Maryland-National Capitol Park and Planning Commission.

86. Surratt, J.H. 1870.

87. Jones, T.A. 1893. J. Wilkes Booth An Account of His Sojourn in Southern Maryland after the Assassination of Abraham Lincoln, his Passage Across the Potomac, and his Death in Virginia. Laird & Lee, Publishers. Chicago, Illinois. 126 pp.

88. Oldroyd, O.H. 1901. The Assassination of Abraham Lincoln. Private printing, Washington D.C. 305 pp.

89. Smoot, R.M. 1908. The Unwritten History of the Assassination of Abraham Lincoln. W.J. Coulter, Clinton, Miss. Republished by Leopold Classic Library. 24 pp.

90. Jones, T. A. 1893.

91. Oldroyd, O.H. 1901.

92. Fisher, G.P. Hon. Presiding. 1867. Transcripts of the trial of John Harrison Surratt. Testimony of Louis Weichmann.

93. Surratt, J.H. 1870.

94. Lee, E.G. General C.S.A. Diary of Edwin Gray Lee. Unpublished microfilm. James O. Hall Research Center. The Maryland-National Capitol Park & Planning Commission. File copy.

95. Jones, J.B. 1866. A Rebel War Clerk's Diary. J.B. Lippincott & Co. Philadelphia, Pennsylvania. 482 pp.

96. Boutwell, G.S. 1865. Assassination of Lincoln. Report of House of Representatives. No. 104. 41 pp.

97. Smoot, R.M. 1908.

98. Fisher, G.P. Hon. Presiding. 1867. Trial of John H. Surratt in the Criminal Court for the District of Columbia. Washington Government Printing Office. Testimony of Eddy Martin. 678 pp.

99. Poore, B.P., ed. 1865.

100. Fisher, G.P., Hon. Presiding. 1867. Testimony of Louis Weichmann.

101. Mosby, John S. 1917. The Memoirs of Colonel John S. Mosby. Ed. By Charles Wells Russell. Little, Brown, and Company. Boston, Mass. 414 pp.

102. Conrad, T., Captain C.S.A. 1904. The Rebel Scout. The National Publishing Company. Washington City. 232 pp.

Brigadier General Edwin Gray Lee in civilian dress shortly after his arrival in Montreal in March of 1865. William Notman photograph, McCord Museum, Photograph I-17037.1.

Michael O'Laughlen was recruited to the kidnapping conspiracy by John Wilkes Booth in August 1864. Civil War Photographs, 1861-1865, Library of Congress, LOT 4195, LC-B817-7783.

Samuel Arnold, recruited in August of 1864, was the most challenging conspirator for John Wilkes Booth to manage. Library of Congress, LOT 4195, LC-B817-7778.

Confederate spy, John Harrison Surratt, carried messages from Washington to Richmond and Richmond to Canada before and during the months that he was Booth's chief co-conspirator. Library of Congress, LOT 4195, No. 9.

Lewis Powell, alias Lewis Paine, added more than just muscle to the team of conspirators. His courage commanded a measure of respect from his Yankee captors. Library of Congress, LOT 4195, B817-7775.

David Herold, who knew the backroads of southern Maryland, was recruited to the conspiracy to kidnap by John H. Surratt. Library of Congress, LOT 4195, B817-7784.

George Atzerodt knew how to row the Potomac River and was recruited to the conspiracy to kidnap by John H. Surratt. Library of Congress, LOT 4195, no. 11.

Confederate spy, Thomas Harbin, assisted John H. Surratt in buying the boat intended to ferry a captured Abraham Lincoln across the Potomac River. Public domain, digital image through the Surratt House Museum/ MNCPPC.

Louis Weichmann exercised his strong sense of self-preservation throughout the manhunt and trial of the conspirators. Public domain image, originally published in The Assassination of Abraham Lincoln Flight, Pursuit, Capture, and Punishment of the Conspirators. 1901.

Had the March 17th kidnapping attempt successfully transported Abraham Lincoln across the Potomac River, Col. John Singleton Mosby (standing, second from left) and members of the 43rd Virginia Cavalry Battalion would then become involved. Other than general readiness, these soldiers likely were ignorant of these and related efforts. Library of Congress, LOT 4210, no. 15.

Abraham Lincoln escaped the heat, humidity and chaos of Washington City with late afternoon retreats to this cottage on the grounds of Soldiers' Home. This habit, observed by Thomas Conrad, greatly enhanced Lincoln's vulnerability to kidnapping. Library of Congress, LOT 12253.

CHAPTER FIVE

Deo Vindice

JANUARY 11–FEBRUARY 17, 1865

CANADIAN JUDGE James Smith's 30-day court recess allowed Southern authorities time to obtain proof that the St. Albans raiders were Confederate soldiers and not subject to extradition to the United States. Government clerks, political leaders and attorneys were expected to coordinate and complete the defense in two weeks. Confederate couriers might need two more to transfer the documents from Richmond.

But there was a problem. Bureaucrats in Richmond received no advanced warning of the court requests. And while the raiders were important to the Confederate government, there were scenarios unfolding that directly threatened Richmond, the makeup of Jeff Davis' cabinet and the government's survival. St. Albans and other missions directed by the Department of the North were not top billing.

Meanwhile, federal detectives knew that Rebel spies would be making runs from Montreal to Richmond to obtain the paperwork. They monitored suspicious people staying at St. Lawrence Hall, tailed them when leaving the hotel, and noted names and addresses of residences they visited in the city as possible safe houses.[103] Detectives also watched anyone who came into contact with them. They were at train depots in Montreal and Toronto. Confederate agents countered by monitoring known and likely federal detectives. After four years of war, including six months of intelligence and counterintelligence experience in Canada, both sides were much improved at this art.

Mrs. Slater agreed to go to Richmond and pick up the needed documents in the St. Albans case and bring them back to Montreal to be placed in evidence. She could leave St. Lawrence Hall, slip past the detectives and hope no one followed her onto the train out of Montreal, or she could take a carriage 15 miles to St. Albans and board the train there. She opted to board the train in Montreal, then go south.

She knew detectives might be on board or waiting to arrest her at any stop along the way, or in New York City or Baltimore while changing trains. Detectives might be watching to see if she talked to anyone. A known spy could yield multiple arrests for patient investigators.

But Mrs. Slater was prepared. She looked French and spoke the language[104]—an excellent skill for a spy headed south out of the French-speaking part of Canada. Fluent French and natural good looks were two attributes that got her started in this business. Audacity and smarts were two more that kept her in it. She could claim to be a citizen of France if need be.[105]

The risks were huge. Confederate spy Lt. Samuel B. Davis left Toronto for Richmond at the time of her departure from Montreal and was caught in Ohio. His trial and sentencing to hang were completed within three days of his being caught.[106] (President Lincoln later intervened in the case, which had become high profile in the United States and Canada. Consequently, Davis was never executed.)

Meanwhile, Mrs. Slater moved with speed, making Richmond in just four days, and noticed everyone there seemed exceptionally worried. Rumors about evacuation of the Confederate capital were rampant.[107] Inside the Confederate War Department, there were other distractions, the latest being that Secretary James Seddon was going to resign.[108]

But Mrs. Slater had no time to worry about it. She had to get the documents quickly and also needed a solid cover story, a believable and documented lie of her own, to get back safely to Montreal. She decided to get official travel papers stating she was a Confederate soldier's wife who had to get to New York City to be with her mother.

Mrs. Slater met with N.C. Congressmen B.S. Gaither and J.G. Ramsay, who were happy to meet with a beautiful young woman, married or not. They didn't know they were out of their league with Mrs. Slater. They listened to her story and got her a travel pass.

The Confederate Army and the War Department rarely issued passports to soldiers' wives. But the congressmen sent a passport request for her to the Richmond provost marshal allowing Mrs. Slater to visit her mother in New York. This initiated her multi-layered Confederate government paper trail and cover story. It documented a reason for her business at the War Department should the wrong eyes notice her.

"House of Representatives
January 16, 1865

Sir:
We have the honor to ask for a passport for Mrs. Nettie Slater of Salisbury, North Carolina, to pass the military lines of the Confederate States. She is a resident of Salisbury but her mother is a French lady residing in the city of New York and her daughter desires to return to her mother, where she can be more comfortably situated. She has lost her only brother in the Confederate Army, and we have no hesitation in vouching for her loyalty and her high social position and hope that she will meet with no difficulty in passing the lines of our army.

We have the honor to be,
Your Obt. St.
B.S. Gaither MC
J.G. Ramsay MC"[109]

The provost marshal in turn forwarded the request with his recommendation of approval to the War Department:

> *"Respy referred to Hon Sec of War. My only reason for hesitating in giving this pass is that the husband of the applicant is in the Confederate service. The representations of Hon Mssrs Gaither & Ramsay make a case for exception to the general rule.*
>
> *I.H. Carrington*
> *Jany 16/65"*[110]

She now had her well-documented lie. Her application stated that she had lost her only brother to disease while he was serving in the Confederate Army. Actually, she had two other brothers who had been in North Carolina's home guard, but they were alive and well. Both had deserted.

Meanwhile, Commissioners Thompson and Clay were nervous. Mrs. Slater had not yet returned from Richmond with the paperwork, but Cameron, who left after her departure on another mission to Virginia, was back. He made it to Richmond in four days, stayed four days and took four more on the return leg, arriving in Montreal on the morning of January 21.

In Richmond, sleet gave way to brutal cold,[111] and the city's trees bent under the weight of ice, but unlike the freezing Confederate soldiers in trenches 20 miles to the south, Mrs. Slater could stay warm while waiting days for the clerks to finish gathering documents in support of the raiders' case.

Meanwhile in Montreal, Edwin Gary Lee and his wife completed their grueling trip across east Canada and checked into St. Lawrence Hall.[112] As the new department chief, Lee was quickly oriented to Montreal operations. On January 23, the Lees boarded a train for Toronto and met with Commissioner Thompson, who Lee knew only by reputation.[113]

Lee handed the dispatch to Thompson, who was not surprised by the visitor or the message. It contained the extracted quotation from the dispatch that he had received almost two weeks previously from agent Cameron: "The political objectives contemplated at the time of your (Thompson's) departure from Richmond being at an end, the President supposes you may desire to return home, etc."

Thompson had sacrificed significantly for the Confederacy and had no intention of making a personal mistake in the ever-growing gamble for Southern independence. He alone controlled the money that the Confederate government had placed in Canadian banks, and he considered directives from Secretary Benjamin as mere suggestions. Thompson would neither leave Canada nor relinquish control of the money, which was not a bale of Confederate script plummeting in value daily. He controlled a value that exceeded several hundred thousand U.S. dollars, albeit in British pounds sterling.

Still, time was running out. Would Mrs. Slater make it back before the extradition proceedings resumed? What if she was arrested on the way back? Thompson, Clay and now Lee turned to agent Steven Cameron, who was available to again go to Richmond.

Meanwhile in and around Virginia, the Confederate civilian government, Signal Corps and related secret service operations required a considerable number of covert passages to move people and information between Richmond and Washington. A Union gunboat could steam up to 16 miles per hour while a rowboat could make only a third of that speed. In the event of a daylight crossing, federal gunners could easily sink a rowboat from a mile away. At night, they could flash reflected light across the dark water to spot small craft. But difficulty crossing the Potomac was not the reason for Mrs. Slater's delay.

It wasn't until January 31 that Mrs. Slater secured the raiders' muster roll with the Great Seal of the Confederate States affixed, proving the men were participating in a military operation at St. Albans. But they were not tiny photographs on the back of a button or written on silk and sewed into a collar or letters interlined in imperceptible ink. These were official documents—full-sized and bulky.[114] The only cover she had to throw off inquisitive federal detectives was the letter signed by the Confederate congressmen and her Confederate States pass to go to New York.

Mrs. Slater left Richmond at dawn on February 1 along with Confederate agent Gus Howell, and the next day in Westmoreland County, Virginia, they met up with agent James Fowle—who had escorted Nettie on her first mission to Montreal. Stephen Cameron, who left Montreal on January 31, arrived in Richmond on February 3, and on February 5 he had duplicates of the raiders' paperwork and headed back to Canada.[115]

On February 3, Confederate peace commissioners quietly met with Lincoln and Stanton about bringing an end to the war. This signaled a desperate shift in the Confederacy's insistence on complete victory and posed a huge political risk for Southern leadership. But three days later, the U.S. Congress passed the 13th Amendment, which abolished slavery throughout the United States, and optimism for a Union victory, absent a year earlier, took firm hold in the North.

Also at that time James Seddon resigned as secretary of war and word was out that he would be replaced on February 6 by John C. Breckinridge, the U.S. vice president from Kentucky prior to Lincoln's election. Breckenridge was expelled from the U.S. Senate when he joined the Confederate Army. News of the transition fueled rumors that the South was about to lose the war.

John Surratt was in the parlor of his mother's boarding house in Washington on February 6 composing a letter to a cousin. It was mostly small talk: He planned to attend a big party on February 11 and joked that Miss Honora Fitzpatrick was in the room along with his sister and playing with a cat in her lap—a sure sign of becoming an old maid. He wrote that he laughed when Honora suddenly began "hustling, bustling and primping"—the cat no longer of much interest—because famous actor John Wilkes Booth was at the door. But Surratt did not note to his cousin that Booth wasn't there for a social visit. He and Surratt had private business to discuss.

On February 11, agent Gus Howell and Mrs. Slater arrived in Washington. Howell stayed at Mary Surratt's boarding house that night, and Mrs. Slater found other accommodations. He visited with the ever-inquisitive boarder Louis Weichmann, who knew Howell only as "Spencer."

Howell showed Weichmann how to use a ciphering machine,[116] explaining that the secret to understanding coded Civil War messages was knowing a key phrase and using the letters in the phrase to translate the message. A month earlier, the Confederacy's 15-letter phrase was "Complete Victory." By February 11 it had been changed to "Come Retribution." It is not known who delivered this key intelligence to the Confederates in Canada.

George Atzerodt arrived at the boarding house that day and John Surratt arrived that evening. Surratt told Atzerodt to room with Howell then left for Toronto, where acquaintances later spotted him in a saloon.

The next morning, Mrs. Slater's carriage arrived in front of the boarding house but she did not get out. Howell exited the house and left with her on a day-long trip to New York City. That evening they registered at the European Hotel. The next day, February 13, she boarded a train bound for Montreal and Howell returned to Mrs. Surratt's house. He was careful to lay low because he was well known to detectives in Washington, having previously been arrested, paroled and exchanged there.

Despite Mrs. Slater's four-day head start over Stephen Cameron, he arrived in Montreal from New York two days ahead of her. She checked in at St. Lawrence Hall at 3 a.m. on February 16 and registered for Room 138 as Mrs. N. Slater from New York.[117] Cameron, not Mrs. Slater, gave his deposition on February 15 in support of the raiders when their case resumed in Canadian superior court. He began by telling his history as a citizen of Maryland and chaplain in the Confederate service, and swore to the following:

> *"... I called on the President (Jefferson Davis), by appointment, and asked that, to insure the safe delivery of the papers, I might be entrusted with a duplicate as a second messenger. He (Davis) readily acquiesced, and expressed great anxiety ... (the papers) are precisely in the same condition now as when I received them ..."*[118]

The U.S. counsel and others present didn't know about the other set of duplicates arriving in Montreal, and they had no idea who it was that checked in at the hotel as Mrs. N. Slater from New York. Cameron identified himself in his deposition as being a Confederate courier. His future in covert operations would be limited as a result. But they were not over because his alias as T.F. Hendrickson was not disclosed.

Mrs. Slater also continued to work undercover for the Confederate States of America. On February 17 she was on her way back to Richmond via New York City with new dispatches for Judah Benjamin, while to her west another spy left Toronto also headed south. Espionage was about to become intensely personal for Mrs. Slater and John Harrison Surratt.

Literature Cited – Chapter Five

103. Fisher, G.P. Hon. Presiding. 1867. Trial of John H. Surratt in the Criminal Court for the District of Columbia. Washington Government Printing Office. Testimony of L.J.A. McMillan. 678 pp.

104. Poore, B.P., ed. 1865. Conspiracy trial for the murder of the president, and the attempt to overthrow the government by the assassination of its principal officers. Testimony of Louis J. Weichmann. J.E. Tilton and Company. Boston, Massachusetts. 1,577 pp.

105. Ibid.

106. Hooker, J. General. 1865. General Order No. 4.

107. Jones, J.B. 1866. A Rebel War Clerk's Diary. J.B. Lippincott & Co. Philadelphia, Pennsylvania. 482 pp.

108. Ibid.

109. Hall, J.O. 1982. The Saga of Sarah Slater. Reprinted in "In Pursuit Of ..." 1990. Compiled from newsletters of the Surratt Society. 292 pp.

110. Ibid.

111. Jones, J. B. 1866.

112. St. Lawrence Hall Register. 1864-65. Unpublished microfilm. James O. Hall Research Center. Maryland-National Capitol Park and Planning Commission. File copy.

113. Levin, A.L. 1987. "This Awful Drama." Vantage Press, Inc. New York, New York. 248 pp.

114. Headley, J. W., Captain C.S.A. 1906. Confederate Operations in Canada and New York. Deposition of Stephen F. Cameron. The Neale Publishing Company.

115. Fisher, G P. Hon. Presiding. 1867. Trial of John H. Surratt in the Criminal Court for the District of Columbia. Washington Government Printing Office. Testimony of Stephen Cameron. 678 pp.

116. Poore, B.P., ed. 1865. Testimony of Louis J. Weichmann.

117. St. Lawrence Hall Register. 1864-65.

118. Headley, J.W., Captain C.S.A. 1906. Deposition of Stephen F. Cameron.

Mrs. Mary E. Surratt supported John Wilkes Booth and Lewis Powell in late March and early April and paid a terrible price for her involvement. Courtesy of Surratt House Museum/ MNCPPC.

Mary Surratt's H Street boarding house served as a Confederate safehouse providing secure lodging for Nettie Slater, Gus Howell, James Fowle, Lewis Powell, and her son John. But, this safehouse had eyes and ears, primarily in the form of Louis Weichmann. Library of Congress, LC-DIG-cwpbh-03432.

CHAPTER SIX

Richmond and Back

February 18–March 9, 1865

ON FEBRUARY 18 in New York City, Kate Brown strolled along Broadway looking for a man she didn't know. She was young and attractive,[119] and wore a black dress and veil—a widow's mask that obscured the fine details of her face. Several gentlemen took notice of her as she passed them by. The veil didn't hide her figure. Young, grieving widows out and about were not uncommon in such troubled times. But "Kate Brown" was no widow. She was Confederate spy Nettie Slater, hiding in plain sight.[120]

She soon saw a tall, slim, well-dressed man about her age who held a switch with a red ribbon on the handle. His goatee neither enhanced his natural good looks nor hid his youth. Mrs. Slater was looking for just such a man carrying a switch with red ribbon attached. The sign was subtle but clear.[121] She stopped and spoke to John Harrison Surratt, recently arrived in New York City from Toronto. They soon left New York together for Washington.

Upon arrival in Washington, Nettie signed in at the National Hotel and Surratt went to Howard's Stable on G Street where he rented a horse and carriage.[122] This was not unusual. Surratt and his mother often rented or borrowed a horse and carriage as needed—usually to travel south of the city to the tavern Mary owned in Surrattsville (now Clinton) or farther to Port Tobacco on a tributary to the Potomac River.

But this time Surratt alone drove the carriage from Howard's Stable to the National Hotel, picked up Mrs. Slater and then went to his mother's boarding house. Upon arrival, he got out of the carriage while she stayed inside. Lewis Weichmann heard that a woman was out front in the carriage but didn't not see her.

Confederate spy James Fowle was also staying at the boarding house, as was Gus Howell.[123] Fowle soon joined Mrs. Slater inside the carriage[124] while Howell took the reins and drove them 40 miles to Port Tobacco. George Atzerodt had joined them too, but he was not in the carriage. He rode a horse alongside.

After Surratt left the carriage, he had told Atzerodt to get the horse from Howard's Stable and accompany the threesome to Port Tobacco. Surratt had informed the proprietor that Atzerodt was authorized to use one of the horses Booth had paid to be boarded there.[125]

It was almost dark on the evening of February 21 when Fowle, Howell, Atzerodt and Mrs. Slater arrived in Port Tobacco. The weather was pleasant, and they did not have to wait long to make the river crossing. Atzerodt knew where the boat was hidden and rowed them to the other side.[126] Fowle, Howell and Mrs. Slater got out in Westmoreland County, Virginia, and Atzerodt rowed back across the Potomac. The trio of spies traveled overland across the Northern Neck of Virginia to Port Royal, where they took a ferry across the Rappahannock River. They took the road to Bowling Green, where they boarded a Potomac Railroad train to Richmond. The route and varying modes of transportation were well known to all three by now. It was the sixth time Nettie had taken it in one direction or the other. Atzerodt returned to Port Tobacco. He drove the horse and carriage and trailed his mount back to Howard's Stable.

Later, during the trial of the eight conspirators accused of taking part in Lincoln's assassination, it was confirmed that Surratt had secured a horse and a carriage from Howard's Stable, but there was no evidence that a woman was with him. By that time, Atzerodt had confessed on two occasions that the woman in the carriage was named either Kate Brown or Kate Thompson. Investigators apparently had no idea who she really was.

In 1866, when U.S. authorities were gathering information regarding prosecuting former Confederate President Jefferson Davis for treason, James Fowle confirmed to a congressional committee that he saw Mrs. Slater in front of Mary Surratt's boarding house, later in Westmoreland County and also in Richmond. But this added nothing more than what others had already told investigators. He also testified that anything they might have said to each other was casual in nature. He said nothing about working with her in Canada.[127]

Mrs. Slater and Howell were in Richmond only a few days after arriving in late February, and the situation there was grim. Gen. Grant was pressing his military advantage, and Rebel agent Thomas Conrad reported to the new Confederate Secretary of War that 35,000 U.S. troops under the command of Gen. George H. Thomas had moved down the Potomac[128] to join Grant's already overwhelming force. Time was running short for Confederate Gen. Robert E. Lee.

Also, N.C. authorities had sent gold from Charlotte to Richmond, but President Davis and Secretary Benjamin had no plans to take it with them when the government relocated to North Carolina.[129] The gold was sent there to help the Confederacy pay debts and cover immediate expenses. The only good news for them at that time was Col. Mosby had returned to active duty and was in Richmond on February 24.[130] The Confederacy needed him and his men more than ever to be at their best.

One hundred miles to the north, President Lincoln was busy writing his second inaugural address, which included stern words for the South: "God may will the war continue until every drop of blood drawn by the lash shall be paid by another drawn by the sword."[131] His resolve was unmistakable, and the Confederate leaders knew it.

As rain fell on Gen. Lee and his army, Mrs. Slater and Howell were on their way back to Washington.[132] They arrived on March 3, and their timing was fortunate. A U.S. flotilla conducted a sweep of the Potomac one day after their crossing. Surratt and Weichmann were out and about in the city that day listening to music and dining on oysters. Later, Surratt left Weichmann saying he had a meeting to attend. When Weichmann got back to the boarding house, he saw Surratt there talking to Booth, but could not hear what they were saying.[133]

On March 4, Booth attended Lincoln's second inauguration. Lucy Hale, a daughter of Sen. John P. Hale of New Hampshire, had secured a pass for him to enjoy the festivities. Lucy and Booth were secretly engaged to be married. She brought to their relationship a standing generally not available to actors, and Booth liked the prestige. More attractive women were available to him elsewhere, but he sincerely enjoyed her companionship. Booth was standing very close to President Lincoln that day and heard his every word:

> *"With malice toward none, with charity for all, with firmness in the right as God gives us to see the right, let us strive on to finish the work we are in, to bind up the nation's wounds, to care for him who shall have borne the battle and for his widow and his orphan, to do all which may achieve and cherish a just and lasting peace among ourselves and with all nations." Abraham Lincoln.*[134]

Lincoln's magnanimity was lost on Booth, who focused only on the President's threat to spill as much blood as might be required to win the war.

John Surratt had more pressing business to attend to that day. Mrs. Slater needed an escort to New York City, and he planned to go to Baltimore for a meeting at Preston Parr's china shop. He agreed to accompany the dark-eyed beauty at least that far on her trip to New York. Parr and Surratt had known each other for a couple of years. Parr's shop was where Surratt often left and received sensitive telegrams.[135] The shop was also a gathering place for other Confederate agents. Parr was a nervous type—excitable under pressure—but he trusted Surratt and was intensely loyal to the Confederacy.

When Surratt arrived at the front door of the shop that day, he spoke briefly with Parr,[136] saying said he wanted him to arrange a meeting a certain gentleman who had been in Baltimore since January. Parr agreed to contact the man (Lewis Powell), who was staying at 16 North Eutaw St., the boarding house operated by Mary and Maggie Branson's mother. Parr went there and arranged the meeting.

Later, Surratt and a woman (probably Mrs. Slater) arrived at the shop along with Lewis Powell, who was with another woman (probably Mary Branson). The ladies were introduced to each other and chatted while admiring china. The men spoke about more serious matters regarding the planned kidnapping. The women's identities were never confirmed, but they surely overheard parts of the men's conversation.

Surratt could have been in the shop that day with a woman other than Mrs. Slater. But another woman's name has not been confirmed in the last 155 years. What has been confirmed is Mrs. Slater was with Surratt and Howell when she passed through Baltimore on her way to New York City at that time. More than likely she went with Surratt that day to Parr's shop.

Parr, in a later statement to detectives about the woman who was with Surratt, claimed to have taken little notice of her. But he did observe that she was around 20 years old with a rather slight frame.[137] Given the sensitive nature of the meeting between Surratt and Powell, the level of trust in this woman was unquestioned by them. Nettie Slater fit the physical description and commanded that level of trust.

As for the identity of the woman with Lewis Powell, there are two possibilities. He was a new arrival in Baltimore and knew no one except the Branson sisters. One of them he appeared to love, and with the other he had formed a closeness like that of a sister. But when Powell was seen by others in Baltimore, he was with Mary, according to later testimony. The level of trust in Miss Branson also was beyond question.

Regarding Mrs. Slater, she could have gone straight to New York City with agent Howell. She was very careful, and meeting with strangers at a Baltimore china shop would have been out of character. If the ladies there that day were Mary and Maggie Branson, Parr's statement saying one asked about the other was a ruse to steer detectives away from the Branson sisters, who Parr knew well. Regardless, Mrs. Slater did go to New York City and on to Montreal, and Surratt returned to Washington.

On March 6, U.S. sailors swept the Rappahannock River while Union attacks on Confederate Signal Corps camps on the Virginia side of the

Potomac River took shape.[138] Federal forces missed no opportunity to probe weaknesses of the crumbling Confederacy at that time.

That night in Richmond, boxes arrived at the War Department to be filled with documents critical to Confederate archives and quickly readied for relocation to North Carolina. Persistent rumors about the immediate evacuation of the capital continued, although authorities maintained that such talk was false. Still, the entire government needed to be on trains and ready to roll without the public any wiser before Lee's withdrawal from Petersburg.

The timing of the government move would telegraph the timing of the military move if Grant got wind of it from excited civilians. A major frontal assault by federal forces when Confederate trenches were being evacuated would be the disaster that would put an end to the army of Northern Virginia. The Confederate government could not begin pulling out too early; their evacuation had to be just prior Gen. Lee's withdrawal. The date was not yet chosen, but once it was, Lee wanted Grant to awaken the next morning and realize that the enemy had stolen a march on him, south and west beyond his left flank, and that no Rebels remained to his front.

Back in Baltimore, the conspirators had problems. Powell lost his temper in Mrs. Branson's boarding house after he told a young maid to clean his room and she refused. Another servant, Margaret Kaighn, later testified that she was taken aback by the rapidly escalating exchange:

"He asked her to clean his room, and she gave some impudence, and said she wouldn't do it. She called him some names, then he slapped her and struck her. He threw her to the ground and stomped on her and said he would kill her."[139] The girl left the house and went to federal authorities. Powell was arrested soon afterward and held for a couple of days.

Union Lt. H.B. Smith suspected Powell was a spy and pressed for corroborating evidence,[140] but he had no idea that he was part of the Lincoln conspiracy. Powell was surly and evasive, but he was not stupid, although he was comfortable letting Lt. Smith think that he was.

At 11:30 p.m. on March 9 in Montreal, Mrs. Slater arrived at St. Lawrence Hall and registered as "A. Reynaud" from New York before retiring to Room 181.[141]

Literature Cited – Chapter Six

119. Chaconas, J.L. 1988. Statement of George A. Atzerodt to Prov. Mar. McPhail in Presence of John L. Smith on the Night of May 1, 1865. Surratt Courier. A Publication of the Surratt Society &The Maryland-National Capitol Park & Planning Commission.

120. Ibid.

121. Fisher, G.P. Hon. Presiding. 1867. Trial of John H. Surratt in the Criminal Court for the District of Columbia. Washington Government Printing Office. Testimony of Louis Weichmann. 678 pp.

122. Chaconas, J.L. 1988.

123. Poore, B.P., ed. 1865. Conspiracy trial for the murder of the President, and the attempt to overthrow the government by the assassination of its principal officers. Testimony of Gus Howell. J.E. Tilton and Company. Boston, Massachusetts.

124. Boutwell G.S. 1866. Assassination of Lincoln. Report of the House of Representatives. No. 104. 41 pp.

125. Poore, B.P., ed. 1865. Conspiracy trial for the murder of the President, and the attempt to overthrow the government by the assassination of its principal officers. Testimony of Brooke Stabler. J.E. Tilton and Company. Boston, Massachusetts.

126. Poore, B.P., ed. 1865. Testimony of Gus Howell.

127. Boutwell G.S., 1866.

128. Jones, J.B. 1866. A Rebel War Clerk's Diary. J.B. Lippincott & Co. Philadelphia, Pennsylvania. 482 pp.

129. Ibid.

130. Mosby, John S., 1917. The Memoirs of Colonel John S. Mosby. Ed. By Charles Wells Russell. Little, Brown and Company. Boston, MA. 414 pp.

131. Lincoln, A. ,1865. Second inaugural address. Library of Congress. Digital Reference Section.

132. Jones, J.B. 1866.

133. Fisher, G.P. Hon. Presiding. 1867. Testimony of Louis Weichmann.

134. Lincoln, A., 1865. Second inaugural address.

135. Parr, P., 1865. Statement given to federal investigators April 26. National Archives. LAS file. M-599, Reel 5.

136. Ibid.

137. Ibid.

138. Smith, H.B. 1915. Between the Lines Secret Service Stories Told Fifty Years After. Booz Brothers. New York, New York. 343 pp.

139. Poore, B.P., ed. 1865. Conspiracy trial for the murder of the President, and the attempt to overthrow the government by the assassination of its principal officers. Testimony of Margaret Kaighn. J.E. Tilton and Company. Boston, Massachusetts.

140. Smith, H.B. 1915.

141. St. Lawrence Hall Register. 1864-65. Unpublished microfilm. James O. Hall Research Center. Maryland-National Capitol Park and Planning Commission. File copy.

CHAPTER SEVEN

Courage and Corruption

MARCH 1–12, 1865

TWO WEEKS after disclosing in a Canadian court that he was a Confederate courier, Stephen Cameron was still in Montreal and being watched by federal detective A.B. Newcomb. The preacher-turned-known-spy was safe as long as he stayed in Canada. The risks he had taken the previous month going to and from Richmond had been huge. But he considered it his sacred duty to keep the St. Albans raiders out of the hands of the U.S. government.[142] He was convinced the federal authorities were inhumane and believed extradition would result in a humiliating execution for Lt. Bennett Young and, most likely, the others. Years later he wrote:

> *"Perhaps no contest in the world ever afforded similar opportunities for acts of individual daring than did the late embittered feud between North and South, and in no department was there more scope for the exercise of adroit courage than was afforded by the Secret Service."*[143]

On the afternoon of March 1, 1865, Cameron caught up on his mail, both reading and writing letters. One of the letters that he wrote was addressed to John Harrison Surratt.[144]

The next day Cameron met with Commissioner Thompson about the direct, enumerated instructions sent from Confederate Secretary of State Judah Benjamin. First, Benjamin wrote, "Use up to $10,000 to assist escaped prisoners as may need aid to return to the Confederacy …" Second, "Advance no more financial resources to Dr. Kensey Stewart." Third, he instructed Thompson to pay $20,000 to his recently arrived replacement, Edwin G. Lee. Fourth, "Reserve enough funding to pay your expenses here to Richmond." Fifth, "Remove the balance of the money to Fraser, Trenholm & Company of Liverpool" for placement in a separate account controlled by Secretary of State. Sixth, he was told to procure relevant court records, and finally, "Return to the Confederacy as fast as you can."[145]

A lot was happening among the Confederates in Canada, and much of it was about money, including Benjamin's seven-point list of finance-related instructions to Thompson. On March 11, Thompson registered in a room at St. Lawrence Hall and paid Gen. E.G. Lee his $20,000 allowance. Thompson forwarded two "favors" with sufficient funds when combined with a draft from Gilipin, Mills & Company of London to cover three warrants payable to Fraser, Trenholm & Company, and left a suitable balance as sought by Benjamin—suitable as Thompson saw things, that is.[146]

For Thompson, it was obvious Benjamin and other Confederate leaders in Richmond were hedging bets concerning the outcome of the war. He decided that the transactions assured the availability of resources if they relocated to Europe with the collapse of the Confederacy. It's also noteworthy that "sufficient" money to secure Thompson's future, more than $200,000, remained in Canadian banks and under his control. Thompson had previously paid agent John Porterfield $23,664; agent George Sanders, $6,000; and agent Lewis Sanders, George Sanders' son, $13,363[147] for their services.

By March 11, Confederate agents Edwin Gary Lee, George Sanders, Beverly Tucker, William Cleary and James Gordon were at St. Lawrence

Hall, too.[148] The Department of the North had gathered there from across Canada. Gordon, who had registered at the hotel on March 8, was lucky to be in Montreal after being arrested upon his return from Europe as his ship sailed into Fort Fisher, N.C., just days after its occupation by Union forces. He was released in Maryland on February 21 because federal authorities misidentified him. From there he went to New York City then on to Canada.

Thompson's banking business was not the only reason for agents of the Department of the North to meet. Everyone knew that something big had to happen quickly to save the Confederate States of America. In addition, some of them were aware that Booth and Surratt were in Washington and working to kidnap Abraham Lincoln. If the kidnapping plan was to be of any value to the war effort, Booth and Surratt did not have much time, and an alternative plan might be needed.

There were other Confederates in Montreal who were lower in rank and profile but certainly not insignificant. They included a double agent—of sorts. Sanford Conover outwardly cooperated with Confederates in Canada while secretly writing for newspapers in New York City. Working under the alias James W. Wallace, he held the confidence of many of the Rebels in Montreal. Actually, Sanford Conover was also an alias, but the Confederates didn't know it. His real name was Charles A. Dunham.

Later, in his testimony at the trial of the conspirators, Conover said he was present in Montreal when Thompson read a dispatch from Richmond, and that in reaction to it, the commissioner said this makes "the thing" alright. Conover indicated that "the thing" that was approved by the Confederacy's top leadership was the assassination of Lincoln.[149] But his testimony was later disputed and he was convicted of perjury.

However, Conover's entire testimony should not be discounted. He gave a lot of accurate details, including independently confirmed dates of Confederate agents' comings and goings in Montreal—especially those of Booth and Surratt. Thompson's phrasing of "the thing" might not be true, or it might have been said within the context of kidnapping rather than assassination, then enhanced after the fact by Conover, who was given to sensational reporting in newspapers as well as his testimony.

While it was somewhat inconspicuous, the phrasing of "the thing" also appeared in one of Atzerodt's confessions. In his late-evening statement to Provost Marshal James McPhail and John Smith on May 1, Atzerodt stated, "Booth said during the day that *the thing* had failed and proposed to go to Richmond and open the theatre." The day referenced was that of the assassination. Atzerodt, a German immigrant who had poor command of English, probably heard Booth use those words and relayed this to detectives. It is unlikely he would independently discuss kidnapping or assassination in colloquial terms used by Confederates in Canada.

Of all those at the S. Lawrence Hall hotel that week, Edwin G. Lee was most optimistic about a complete victory for the South. This is confirmed in his diary entries after the fall of Richmond, and after Gen. Robert E. Lee's surrender the following week. Edwin Lee, like his famous cousin, held the rank of general in the Confederate Army, and had an excellent understanding of the military realities at that time—certainly more so than the others who gathered at the St. Lawrence Hall—and he believed until the end that the South could win the war.[150] Further evidence of his optimism occurred when he worked on arranging a mass escape of Confederates from the prisoner-of-war camp at Elmira, New York in mid-April.

He obviously disagreed with several Confederate elites at the hotel and also some in Richmond who felt that the Confederacy was, by the early months of 1865, defeated. Despite the emerging defeatism, Colonel James Gordon was willing to return to New York from St. Lawrence Hall and meet with Booth if needed.[151, 152] But Gordon's return to New York was not necessary yet. Mrs. Slater was in Montreal and available for another assignment. She knew John Surratt well by then and was as comfortable with him as he was with her. She was an ideal messenger to deliver and receive communications to still-active Rebel agents in Washington.

Literature Cited – Chapter Seven

142. Cameron, S.F. (presumed author). Date unspecified. Untitled manuscript, Notes for a "History of the Confederate Secret Service." Unpublished. James O. Hall Research Center. The Maryland-National Capitol Park & Planning Commission. File copy. 25 pp.

143. Ibid.

144. Ibid.

145. Ibid.

146. Ibid.

147. Langhorn. 1865. Statement to investigators. National Archives. LAS file. M-599, Reel 6.

148. St. Lawrence Hall Register. 1864-65. Unpublished microfilm. James O. Hall Research Center. Maryland-National Capitol Park and Planning Commission. File copy.

149. Poore, B.P., ed. 1865. Conspiracy trial for the murder of the President, and the attempt to overthrow the government by the assassination of its principal officers. Testimony of Sanford Conover. J.E. Tilton and Company. Boston, Massachusetts. 1577 pp.

150. Lee, E.G. General C.S.A., Diary of Edwin Gray Lee. Unpublished microfilm. James O. Hall Research Center. The Maryland-National Capitol Park & Planning Commission. File copy.

151. Jones, J.B. 1866. A Rebel War Clerk's Diary. J.B. Lippincott & Co. Philadelphia, Pennsylvania. 482 pp.

152. New York Times. December 29, 1909. New Senator Once Fugitive.

CHAPTER EIGHT

Mission Like No Other

MARCH 12–17, 1865

MRS. SLATER left Montreal for Washington early on the morning of March 12 and arrived at midday on March 13. This mission was unlike any she has undertaken before. Previously, she carried ciphered messages or other documents from Canada to the Confederate Departments of State and of War in Richmond, or from those departments back into Canada. Montreal and Richmond anchored each end of her journeys. But this time she was to go to Washington City and immediately return to Montreal.

It was not only Confederate leaders in Canada that understood the situation was desperate. Perhaps Booth did not understand the full measure of desperation, but he certainly felt the pressure. Some of that was self-generated. He was still sorry he did not choose military duty as an expression of his patriotism. Some pressure came from inside his own group—two of whom expressed frustration at having taken no actual steps to kidnap Lincoln. Additional pressure came from clandestine Confederate operatives in New York and those gathered at St. Lawrence Hall. Booth knew he must act soon.

In his confession of May 1, 1865, Atzerodt said Booth knew someone in New York who would attempt to kill Lincoln by exploding a mine under the president and guests at the White House, or when he was at War Department headquarters. "Booth said, 'If he did not get him quick, the New York crowd would.'"[153] More than anything, Booth feared losing his place in history. A telegram sent by Booth to team member O'Laughlen on March 13 and another on March 27 clearly convey his sense of urgency.

Neither Surratt nor Booth missed the significance of a spy's mission from Canada to Washington for their benefit without that person proceeding onto Richmond for other transmittals. They felt the pressure as intended and took immediate action: Booth sent the March 13th telegram to O'Laughlen in Baltimore while Mrs. Slater was still in Washington City: "Don't fear to neglect your business, you had better come at once,"[154,155] he wrote. On March 14, Surratt sent a telegram to Preston Parr: "Immediately telegraph if my friend is disengaged and can see me this evening in Washington." Parr responded, "She will be over on the 6 p.m. train."[156]

O'Laughlen traveled, roomed and drank with co-conspirator Samuel Arnold. They had become close friends after their introduction late in the summer of 1864. Their frustration with the lack of action in the clandestine operation was Booth's biggest challenge as team manager. Booth sent word to O'Laughlen, the less outspoken of the two, to come to the U.S. capital.

O'Laughlen contacted Arnold and together they took the train to Washington to be at Booth's disposal on March 14. That evening a tall young man posing as a Baptist preacher arrived at twilight at Mary Surratt's H Street boarding house. There was no access at the ground level, so he took the outside steps to the second floor. He was the "she" referenced in Preston Parr's telegram—and "she" was Lewis Powell, who posed as "the Rev. Wood."

Powell (aka "Paine"), by no small measure of luck, was also available to Booth. Federal detectives were not so concerned about him beating and threatening to kill the black servant girl. But Lt. Smith did suspect that the surly "Mr. Paine" was a spy. Smith held him an extra day after "Paine" signed another oath of allegiance.[157] Powell's liberty was restored but limited, and he was required to stay north of Washington City and Maryland.

Smith released Powell, who immediately violated the conditions of his release and made the 6 p.m. train from Baltimore to Washington as promised.

He checked in at Mary Surratt's boarding house as the Baptist preacher.[158] The previous time he signed in as a clerk in Parr's china shop.[159]

Mrs. Slater also needed a room on the night of March 14, so that afternoon John Surratt obtained a horse and wagon and drove her to H Street to stay at the boarding house. When she arrived, Mary Surratt asked Weichmann to carry Mrs. Slater's trunk up to his room, which she would use for the night. Since the boarding house was full, Weichmann was told to double up in a back room on the third floor.[160]

Weichmann was accustomed to doubling up when John Surratt was home. He also was attracted to "the pretty widow" even though a black veil covered her facial features. She was pleasant, slight of frame and "sprightly in all her movements."[161] He assisted in getting her to the room, but it was absent an introduction, which disappointed him.

At 11:30 p.m. on March 9 and again at 8 a.m. on March 17, Mrs. Slater checked into St. Lawrence Hall as "A. Reynaud."[162] This was the second and third time at the hotel that she used the initial of her formal name, "Antoinette," and her mother's maiden name. Fine sleuthing by historians uncovered this almost a century and a half after the fact.[163] But they and others have missed the significance of this unique mission and the fact she did not carry correspondence to Richmond.

On March 14, she was known to be in Washington. The date was documented in Weichmann's testimony and bookended by the failed March 17 kidnap attempt and the date and time of her March 9 check-in at St. Lawrence Hall. With these three visits—to Montreal, Washington and Montreal—and precise dates fixed, it is interesting to count available days to eliminate the impossible. There was not enough time between check-ins at St. Lawrence Hall for a mission from Montreal to Richmond and back. Such a trip would take at least eight full days.

She could not have started for Washington before the morning of March 10. She arrived in Montreal during the last 30 minutes of March 9. She then would have had to deliver her dispatches from Richmond, collect other dispatches for Richmond and catch the next train for New York City. Her departure on the morning of March 10 was possible, albeit unlikely.

Her return to St. Lawrence Hall on the morning of March 17 would have taken her, at most, seven days, one full day short. Factoring in the overnight stay in Washington would add at least a half-day. Thus, Nettie's destination this time was Washington. Her documented travel time, including the added overnight layover, would be at least a day and a half short of the minimum required for the longer Richmond mission.

Lost to history is a meeting in Washington she probably had with Booth. But she had been in contact with John Surratt. Multiple people saw them together on March 14 when John drove her to his mother's boarding house. If her mission was to gather intelligence for the Confederate apparatus in Montreal or to deliver a message of urgency regarding Lincoln's kidnapping, meeting with Surratt was as good as meeting with Booth. But if that was the mission, as circumstances and timing of conspirator responses suggest it was, she most likely met with both men. Booth was in the city and available at that time.

Even more telling is the intense activity among Booth and the conspirators directly correlated with the timing of her arrival in Washington on March 13. Two urgent messages went out, one from Booth and one from Surratt, on March 13 and March 14 to three conspirators who were at that time in Baltimore. All of them immediately took the train to Washington. Within one day of Surratt's telegram, Lewis Powell and John Surratt, escorting young ladies who stayed with Mary Surratt, were reconnoitering the president's box at Ford's Theatre.

Around 11 p.m. that night, Booth sent Herold to summon O'Laughlen and Arnold from their hotel to Gautier's Restaurant. All conspirators slated for an initial, active role in the kidnapping—Booth, Surratt, Powell, Herold, Atzerodt, O'Laughlen and Arnold—showed up at Gautier's after Surratt's and Powell's evening of gathering intelligence at Ford's Theatre. A late night of oysters, cards and brandy at Gautier's was the only time all of them were together. And it coincided with the special gathering of the Department of the North elites at St. Lawrence Hall.

Perhaps Mrs. Slater's mission to Washington was to pass along correspondence unrelated to the kidnapping to another Confederate agent, who would carry it to Richmond. But all else happening among the conspirators at that time in Washington would have to be dismissed as a series of coincidences. Surratt would have provided her escort support across town to a secure boarding house that happened to be a little crowded that night. And was it only happenstance that Surratt and Powell were there using the boarding house as a base to reconnoiter alternative kidnapping plans, which included taking Lincoln from his box at Ford's Theatre instead of abducting him on a road to the Soldier's Home.

In addition, a spy dispatching information to another spy was not a documented procedure for Confederate agents operating between Canada and Richmond. It was too risky. But doing so would have allowed Mrs. Slater to rush back to Montreal and wait five days for her next assignment. However, if there had been an immediate need for her to get back to Montreal to move pending dispatches, why didn't she already have them in her possession so she could move on to Richmond from Washington?

The most likely scenario is that Nettie's business in Washington involved the conspiracy to take Lincoln from the city. Authors Tidwell, Hall and Gaddy have since offered a strong argument in their book, "Come Retribution," that the purpose of removing Lincoln as head of government was to create a constitutional crisis and confusion in the federal chain of command just ahead of Robert E. Lee's withdrawal from the Petersburg line.[164] Confusion over the capture of the U.S. commander and chief surely would have added to Lee's odds for success.

Only those present knew the full story: Mrs. Slater was ready to leave Washington. Howell picked her up in front of the boarding house early the next morning. He had been in the city several days awaiting her arrival and planned to escort her to New York City. But she made a rare mistake. In her room, soon to be occupied again by the inquisitive Louis Weichmann, she left a delicate pair of lady's shoes.[165] Weichmann told Mary Surratt about the shoes, and she admonished him about paying so much attention to others' business.

Weichmann was dangerous. He was a pleaser who had been excluded yet knew too much. He was cowardly with a strong sense of self-preservation. He had contacts in the U.S. War Department. He also knew he had been compromised. So, he went to his boss, Capt. Gleason, and told him John Wilkes

Booth was a Confederate sympathizer—which practically everyone already knew. He also told Gleason that unusual people—including a mysterious French widow—had been staying at the boarding house, and that he wondered if people staying there were couriers and blockade runners. He asked if it was possible for someone to kidnap Lincoln. Weichmann was sharing just enough information to appear loyal to the United States to ensure he would not be hanged. Gleason dismissed what he said as so much drivel.

"A. Reynaud" from New York checked into Room 146 of St. Lawrence Hall at 8 a.m. on March 17. That evening department chief Edwin G. Lee noted in his diary: "St. Patrick's Day. Great procession. At 8 p.m. Col. Thompson read his dispatch from Richmond. Extremely interesting—no news."[166] But there was news, although Confederates in Canada and Richmond were not yet aware of it.

March 17 was the day that Booth, Surratt, Powell, Herold, Atzerodt, Arnold and O'Laughlen failed to kidnap Lincoln—thanks to poor intelligence collected by Booth or a change of plans by the president. Lincoln did not attend the benefit performance for wounded soldiers at the hospital. As best the conspirators could determine, U.S. Treasurer Salmon Chase went instead. The conspirators, who at the onset of the March 17 kidnapping attempt were nervous, were now panicky. Do the detectives know something? Was Secretary Chase merely bait for a trap? Are Booth and Surratt being watched?[167] Why didn't the president show?

Yet Booth, Surratt and Powell still planned to kidnap Lincoln.

Literature Cited – Chapter Eight

153. Chaconas, J.L. 1988. Confession of George A. Atzerodt, published in the Baltimore American on January 18, 1869. Surratt Courier. A publication of the Surratt Society & The Maryland-National Capitol Park & Planning Commission.

154. Fisher, G.P. Hon. Presiding. 1867. Trial of John H. Surratt in the Criminal Court for the District of Columbia. Washington Government Printing Office. Pierrepont submission of evidence. 678 pp.

155. Pitman, B., ed. 1865. The Assassination of President Lincoln and Trial of the Conspirators: Compiled and Arranged by Benn Pitman. New York: Moore, Wilsatch, and Baldwin. 423 pp.

156. Parr, P. 1865. Statement given to federal investigators April 26. National Archives. LAS file. M-599, Reel 5.

157. Smith, H.B. 1915. Between the Lines, Secret Service Stories Told Fifty Years After. Booz Brothers. New York, New York. 343 pp.

158. Poore, B.P., ed. 1865. Conspiracy trial for the murder of the President, and the attempt to overthrow the government by the assassination of its principal officers. Testimony of Louis Weichmann. J.E. Tilton and Company. Boston, Massachusetts. 1,577 pp.

159. Fisher, G.P. Hon. Presiding. 1867. Trial of John H. Surratt in the Criminal Court for the District of Columbia. Washington Government Printing Office. Testimony of Louis J. Weichmann. 678 pp.

160. Poore, B.P., ed. 1865. Testimony of Louis Weichmann.

161. Weichmann, L. J. 1975. A True History of the Assassination of Abraham Lincoln and the Conspiracy of 1865. F. E. Risvold, ed. Alfred A. Knopf, Inc. New York, New York. 492 pp.

162. St. Lawrence Hall Register. 1864-65.

163. Stanton, J. F. 2011. A Mystery No Longer: The Lady in the Veil. Surratt Courier. A Publication of the Surratt Society & The Maryland-National Capitol Park and Planning Commission.

164. Tidwell, W.A., J.O. Hall, and D.W. Gaddy. 1988.

165. Weichmann, L.J. 1975.

166. Lee, E. G. General C.S.A. Diary.

167. Surratt, J.H. 1870. Lecture at Rockville, Maryland. Transcript carried in December 7, 1870 edition of the Evening Star newspaper, Washington, D. C.

CHAPTER NINE

Women on the Brain

MARCH 18–APRIL 6, 1865

ON THE MORNING of March 18, the day after the aborted kidnapping, John Surratt and George Atzerodt saddled up and left Washington for Port Tobacco to find Davy Herold, who had been waiting with a boat to take Lincoln across the Potomac into Virginia. But Herold was not there. They found him before reaching that little town on the road back to Washington and carrying the two rapid-fire Spencer rifles, possession of which could have landed them all in prison.

They decided to hide the carbines at John Lloyd's tavern in Surrattsville. Lloyd, who rented the tavern from Mary Surratt, reluctantly agreed to stash the weapons upstairs under a floor joist.[168] Afterwards, Surratt, Herold and Atzerodt left for Washington. Fellow conspirators Sam Arnold and Michael O'Laughlen planned to stay overnight in the city and leave the next day for their return to Baltimore.[169] Powell was headed to Baltimore to see Mary Branson before traveling on to New York City to meet with Surratt, Booth and Southern sympathizers operating from that place.

On the night of March 18 in Washington, Booth headlined his last-ever performance, playing the part of Pescara in "The Apostate," and Surratt,

Herold and Atzerodt were in the audience.[170] The show went well, and Booth stayed for three days in plain sight in the city.[171]

The next day Surratt received a letter from Roderick Dhu Watson, a southern Marylander and Confederate sympathizer despite being employed in New York City's shipping industry. He was part of the covert information network connecting Richmond to Confederate Canada:

"New York
March 19, 1865
Mr. J.H. Surratt

Dear Sir:
I would like to see you on important business if you can spare the time to come to New York. Please telegraph me immediately on the reception of this whether you can come or not & oblige.

Yours &
R.D. Watson

P.S. Address care of Demill & Co.
178½ Water St."[172]

The message appeared normal, but Surratt understood the real meaning: A Confederate courier (Mrs. Slater) needed an escort from New York City to Washington. Would Surratt be available to do the job? Surratt had complete confidence in Watson and planned to make himself available. Gus Howell—who had previously escorted Mrs. Slater—would wait south of the city to take her from Surrattsville across the river to Richmond.

Atzerodt was told to lay low in Washington, but he liked bars and spent a lot of time and most of his money drinking in them. He also liked to talk when drunk. Davy Herold liked to hunt quail in southern Maryland. He could do that or just remain idle and out of sight, but reasonably close to Washington.

On March 21, Booth paid his bill at the National Hotel and left for New York City, where, as planned he met with Surratt and Powell and the

"New York Crowd"—those Southern sympathizers operating in that city. They discussed the failed kidnapping and planned another attempt. Afterward, Surratt returned to Washington before Booth and Powell, and a day ahead of Mrs. Slater's arrival in New York on March 23. Another escort would accompany her to Washington, where Surratt would meet her.

On March 23, Booth sent a telegram to Weichmann: "Tell John (Surratt) to telegraph the number and street at once."[173,174] Booth wanted to arrange housing for Powell in Washington, rather than Baltimore where he could reach Powell for help on short notice when the next kidnapping opportunity arose. Surratt arranged for Powell to stay in a room at the Herndon House at the corner of Ninth and F streets in Washington, just over a block east of Ford's Theatre.[175] He sent the number and street to Booth.

Also that day at the post office, Surratt received a letter addressed to "James Sturdey," which Surratt had told Weichmann was one of his aliases. Weichmann saw that it was sent by a man named Wood from New York.[176] He recalled that Wood was the name of a clerk at a Baltimore china shop, who also had claimed to be a Baptist preacher, and who had stayed at Mary Surratt's boarding house. Weichmann thought all this was odd.

Weichmann and Surratt were often together, and Louis occasionally wrote notes to others on John's behalf. One was about the final payment for the boat that Booth and Surratt planned to use to get Lincoln across the Potomac.[177] Partial payment of the $250, ultimately to go to riverman Richard Smoot, was held in Port Tobacco by an ex-judge named Stone. The boat was stored by local farmer George Bateman. Smoot was eager to be paid for the sale, which occurred more than two months previously.[178]

Surratt got Weichmann to write the note about the boat payment to Smoot and thus further compromised his friend. Weichmann didn't ask what the generic reference to money was about. He was just happy to be included.

Two days earlier on March 21, U.S. Marshal Robert Murray of New York City had reported to Charles Dana, assistant secretary of war, about information gathered by one of his detectives, A.B. Newcombe, who had gone to Montreal to figure out how covert Confederate messages were being sent to Richmond. Newcombe had observed a pretty, 18-year-old woman—known as Miss McGruder—who he thought was carrying the dispatches. He also reported that Rebel agent Stephen Cameron used women dressed as nuns to carry secret mail.[179] Subsequently, federal detectives were told to pay particular attention to women who might be couriers.

Mrs. Slater was unaware of this but was always careful anyway. She did know it was especially important to get messages to Secretary Benjamin in Richmond. In Canada, the new secret service chief, Edwin G. Lee, noted in his diary: "Fixed up and sent letter to Mr. B. ... I pray she may go safely."[180]

Mrs. Slater made it safely to New York City, met her escort and took the overnight train to Washington. Booth happened to be on that train. Although the identity of Mrs. Slater's escort would never be confirmed, it was likely John Wilkes Booth himself. Surratt picked up Mrs. Slater at the National Hotel early on the morning of March 24 in a four-seater carriage pulled by gray horses. He arrived at the boarding house around 7:30 a.m. Mary Surratt joined them on a trip to Surrattsville. Weichmann was downstairs in the dining room having breakfast but saw nothing. But at 8 a.m. another boarder, a Mr. Holahan, saw the fine rig leaving with John, Mrs. Surratt and a pretty young woman on board.[181] At Surrattsville, agent Gus Howell was to meet the carriage and take Mrs. Slater on to Richmond.

Skies were clear but the wind picked up as the trio arrived at Lloyd's Tavern. But Howell wasn't there.[182] The Surratts and Mrs. Slater were told that U.S. cavalrymen had arrested him the previous day and took him to the Old Capitol Prison in Washington.

David Barry, a long-time acquaintance of John Surratt who lived within a mile of Surrattsville, was at the tavern and agreed to ride with John and Mrs. Slater—who was introduced as "Mrs. Brown"—to Port Tobacco. Mrs. Surratt remained at the tavern and planned to catch a ride back to the city.

John Surratt, Mrs. Brown and Barry later stopped at Brawner's Tavern, a gathering spot for local roughs and others passing through Port Tobacco. Barry was an ex-Confederate soldier and well known at Brawner's. Barry noted that Mrs. Brown was slim, delicate, with black eyes and dark hair, under 30 years old, attractive and wore a veil.[183] Gentlemen rarely had difficulty describing her, but never got a good enough look to positively identify her.

Surratt was either going to place Mrs. Slater in care of a capable escort or take her to Richmond himself,[184] although the timing was not good to for him to spend days traveling to and from Richmond no matter how much he admired the company.

Back in Washington, Booth was reassembling his team of conspirators for another attempt at grabbing Lincoln. The pressure on him to act quickly was intense. Spring forage was coming up in the fields for Gen. Robert E. Lee's horses. It also matched anticipated drying of the red-clay roads in Virginia's central piedmont over which Lee's army would march.

These military realities Booth did not understand, but the pressure he understood fully, and the need for immediate action was clear. At that time, Booth told Atzerodt that if he did not get Lincoln soon, "the N. York crowd would."[185] Booth, who certainly didn't want to be upstaged, sent an unusual telegram to O'Laughlen:

> *"Washington, D.C., 27 March 1865.*
>
> *To M. O'Laughlin Esq., 57 North Exeter Street, Baltimore, Md.:*
> *Get word to Sam. Come on, with or without him, Wednesday morning.*
> *We sell that day for sure. Don't fail.*
>
> *J. Wilkes Booth"*[186]

Powell arrived at the Herndon House on Sunday, March 27. Atzerodt and Herold already were in the city.[187] Booth did not know if Arnold would join them because they had parted company after exchanging threats and ultimatums. But Booth assumed John Surratt would be available. Surratt knew that crossing the Potomac with Mrs. Slater and escorting her to Richmond would prevent any communications with Booth until he returned to Washington days later. He opted to go with her, and asked David Barry to return the carriage and team to Brooke Stabler along with his note:

> *"March 26, 1865*
>
> *Mr. Brooke (Stabler):*
> *As business will detain me for a few days in the country, I thought I would*
> *send your team back. Mr. Bearer (Barry) will deliver it safety and pay hire*

on it. If Mr. Booth, my friend, should want my horses, let him have them, but no one else. If you should want any money on them, he will let you have it. I should have liked to have kept the team for several days, but it is too expensive, especially as I have women on the brain, and may be away for a week or two.

Yours respectfully,
J. Harrison Surratt"[188]

After returning the team and carriage to the stable, Barry stopped at the boarding house to tell Mary Surratt that her son had gone on to Richmond with Mrs. Brown. Barry's visit was not a simple courtesy call to a concerned mother. He planned to ask Mrs. Surratt to send a message to Booth about when her son was expected to return. As it happened, Atzerodt and Booth were at the boarding house when Barry arrived. Mrs. Surratt introduced Barry to Booth and the men talked.[189]

Mrs. Slater did not have to read the note to Brooke Stabler about having "women on the brain" to know about Surratt's special interest in her. She enjoyed his admiring glances, which began the last time he escorted her. He was handsome, dashing and daring. Although she was married, she was drawn to Surratt and looked forward to crossing the Potomac with him.

As the sun set on the river, the weather was calm and cold. The boat, crew and passengers shoved off from the Maryland shore as the shadows from the Virginia side met the glare on the water of the Maryland side. The problem with blockade running in that direction at that time of day was the difficulty of seeing out of the sun and into the shadows. While it was difficult for crews on gunboats to spot them, it was also hard for them to see the gunboats. But Mrs. Slater's deliverers were experienced, and she trusted them to get her safely to Virginia.

The blockade runners were well in the shadows before they saw a steamer closing in on them. The crew rowed as hard as they could to reach a tributary on the Virginia side. But the steamer was too fast and the rowboat too heavy. The steamer was close enough for everyone to hear the command: Surrender or be fired upon. The rowing ceased.

The Federals lowered a small craft to reach the rowboat. With as little show as possible, the Confederates made ready. The Yankees pulled close enough to secure ropes when the Rebels opened fire.[190] The blockade runners rowed as hard as they could. Failing light, confusion, limited maneuverability of the gunboat and luck all worked to their advantage. They soon made it to the tributary and the safety of the Virginia shore.

Within a day, Surratt and Mrs. Slater had crossed the Rappahannock River by ferry and reached the railroad tracks to Richmond. They boarded a platform car drawn by black men, and slowly headed south through an area that was not controlled by either army. Surratt and Mrs. Slater surely took comfort in knowing that Col. Mosby's rangers were in the vicinity.

Looking down the tracks, they saw five or six men walking north. As the platform car closed the distance, it became obvious the men were rag-tag Yankee soldiers who were either escaped prisoners or deserters. Mrs. Slater yelled "Shoot the damned Yankees," or something similar,[191] and the Rebels wasted no time opening fire. Black powder smoke hung in the air momentarily. When it cleared, everyone on the platform saw that the Yankees were dead.

On March 29, Surratt checked into Richmond's Spotswood Hotel in time for supper, and registered as "Henry Sherman."[192] Richmond was a nervous town. Inflation was rampant. People were hungry and fearful. Rumors of the government's evacuation persisted. Also that day Gen. Robert E. Lee ordered the sinking of Confederate gunboats at Chaffin's Bluff to obstruct passage by enemy vessels.[193] Lee's plans required slowing the federal advance once he pulled his army from the Petersburg trenches, but Richmond's citizenry were not aware of it.

What they did know was that food was scarce and expensive. Even though American shad were starting their spawning run in tidal rivers, few people in the area possessed the means to catch them. A pair of the seasonally abundant fish cost $50.[194]

Surratt met with Sgt. Harry Brogden, whom he knew from the Signal Corps camp. Brogden had been reassigned from the Signal Corps station near Mathias Point to Richmond. He accompanied Surratt to the Confederate State Department, where they met with Secretary of State Judah Benjamin.

Benjamin told Surratt that Richmond was not to be evacuated, which was a lie. Confederate government records were already packed and ready to move by rail for North Carolina. Benjamin had a Treasury warrant for $1,500 in gold payable to himself on the Secret Service account and had issued other warrants to key officials.[195] If need be, this money would get Benjamin to England, where more money awaited.

He assured Surratt that Richmond was safe, and all was well.[196] Thus, if Surratt was arrested in Maryland or beyond, all he would know and all he could share with federal captors was the Confederacy was staying put in Richmond. Benjamin paid Surratt $200 in gold pieces—compensation sufficient for Mrs. Slater and himself. They left Richmond after breakfast on April 1.[197]

On April 2 the Confederate States Treasury—along with bureaucrats and an escort—left Richmond in two railroad cars for Danville, Virginia. From there, the government planned to relocate to a temporary capital in North Carolina. The Confederacy's wealth rolling on the rails out of Richmond was down to only $200,000, mostly silver and silver bullion. Approximately $300,000 in additional gold, which had been deposited by private individuals in Richmond banks, was also onboard along with Jefferson Davis and his cabinet.[198]

The dramatic change in logistics meant Lincoln's kidnapping was off the table, Booth and his team of kidnappers all but forgotten. Since President Davis and his cabinet were considered legitimate targets for killing under Lincoln's black flag order the previous year, some Confederate authorities believed it was appropriate for the U.S. President as commander in chief of Union forces, to be under a black flag too. In other words, Lincoln's assassination was an option.

Thomas Harney, an explosives expert working for the Confederate Torpedo Bureau, also left Richmond that day. He headed to Washington along the west side of the Potomac River and was escorted by Confederate Marylanders under Col. Mosby's command.

On April 4, Union Col. E.H. Hastings and the 9th Vermont Infantry occupied Richmond not far from the Confederate Torpedo Bureau. A captured Confederate named William H. Snyder, who worked in the bureau, told his captors that a squad had been dispatched on a mission involving explosives and that President Lincoln himself was in danger, but Snyder offered no details because he possessed none. Snyder's story supported information in Atzerodt's later confession about Booth's comment that a "New York crowd" planned to kill Lincoln with an explosion. Snyder's warning to federals and Atzerodt's later statement revealed a backup plan to explode a mine next to the War Department while Lincoln was inside. As of early April 1865, Abraham Lincoln was targeted for assassination by Confederate authorities.

John Surratt and Mrs. Slater took only two and a half days to get from Richmond to Mary Surratt's boarding house in Washington, arriving at 4 p.m. on April 3 via the Leonardtown stagecoach.[199] Mrs. Slater was not traveling light this time. She had two trunks aboard instead of one.

Two days previously, troops under Confederate Gen. George Pickett failed to stop Union forces at Five Forks crossroads southwest of Petersburg. This crossroads Robert E. Lee had ordered Pickett to hold at all hazards. Losing it meant Gen. Lee's Army of Northern Virginia was blocked from going straight to North Carolina. While the butcher's bill for Gen. Pickett's failure this time was not as high as it was on the third day at Gettysburg, it was a disaster equal to or of greater strategic significance. U.S. Gen. Grant capitalized on the Five Forks victory with a massive assault rolling up Lee's right flank. Thus, both armies were engaged and on the move. Instead of retreating south, Lee was forced to detour west. Speed, not secrecy, would determine the outcome.

Meanwhile at Mary Surratt's boarding house in Washington, Weichmann told John Surratt that Richmond had fallen. Surratt was incredulous because Secretary Judah Benjamin insisted the city would be safe. But the Confederate capital was ablaze, and the next day Abraham Lincoln was in Richmond—but not as a kidnapped pawn. He was in the evacuated Confederate capital sitting triumphantly behind Jefferson Davis' desk.

Surratt wanted to talk to Booth, who was no longer in Washington. Surratt also had secret dispatches needed in Montreal that, ironically, he had concealed in a copy of a biography titled "The Life of John Brown."[200] Surratt and Mrs. Slater soon left the city and headed north in search of Booth by way of his brother Edwin, who lived in Maryland. But John Wilkes Booth and his fiancé Lucy Hale were on a train to Rhode Island for a romantic getaway. So Surratt and Mrs. Slater continued north to New York City and Montreal.

On April 6 at 10:30 a.m., Surratt checked into Room 50 at St. Lawrence Hall in Montreal, signing the register as "John Harrison,"[201] and he later delivered the dispatches to department chief Edwin G. Lee. He was now alone. Mrs. Slater had left Surratt when they reached New York City, where she planned to settle down near her mother and sister.

Surratt mentioned the fall of Richmond to Edwin G. Lee and was surprised when Lee was not overly concerned. What Lee knew and Surratt did not was that the evacuation had been under consideration as far back as December when Lee and his wife left for Canada. Lee recognized the timing was right for such a retreat. But he did not know that his famous cousin was running for the life of his Army of Northern Virginia, which had been forced to flee west with Grant in hot pursuit. And Ulysses S. Grant, not Robert E. Lee, controlled the ongoing engagement.

Edwin Lee noted in his journal that he had received the secret dispatch via Surratt, whom he referred to by an alias: "Letter by Charlie from Mr. Benjamin."[202] Lee also noted he was glad to know that Mrs. Slater was OK, adding "my last rec'd all safe."[203] Coincident with the meeting between Surratt and Lee, Commissioner Thompson withdrew $180,000 from the Confederate States account in the Bank of Ontario.[204]

Literature Cited – Chapter Nine

168. Poore, B.P., ed. 1865. Conspiracy trial for the murder of the president, and the attempt to overthrow the government by the assassination of its principal officers. Testimony of John M. Lloyd. J.E. Tilton and Company. Boston, Massachusetts. 1,577 pp.

169. Arnold, S.B. 1865. True copy of written statement given to federal investigators. National Archives. LAS file. M-619, Reel 458.

170. Oldroyd, O.H. 1901. The Assassination of Abraham Lincoln. Private printing, Washington D.C. 364 pp.

171. Poore, B.P., ed. 1865. Conspiracy trial for the murder of the president, and the attempt to overthrow the government by the assassination of its principal officers. Testimony of G.W. Bunker. J.E. Tilton and Company. Boston, Massachusetts. 1,577 pp.

172. Hall, J.O. 1982. The Saga of Sarah Slater. Reprinted "In Pursuit Of ..." 1990. Compiled from newsletters of the Surratt Society. 292 pp.

173. Pitman, B., ed. 1865. The Assassination of President Lincoln and the Trial of the Conspirators: Compiled and Arranged by Benn Pitman. New York: Moore, Wilsatch, and Baldwin. 423 pp.

174. Poore, B.P., ed. 1865. Conspiracy trial for the murder of the president, and the attempt to overthrow the government by the assassination of its principal officers. Testimony of Louis Weichmann. J.E. Tilton and Company. Boston, Massachusetts. 1,577 pp.

175. Pitman, B., ed. 1865.

176. Oldroyd, O.H. 1901.

177. Weichmann, L.J. 1865. Statements given to federal investigators. National Archives. LAS file. M-599. Reel 6.

178. Smoot, R.M. 1908. The Unwritten History of the Assassination of Abraham Lincoln. Press of W. J. Coulter, Clinton, Massachusetts. 24 pp.

179. Murray, R. 1865. Report given to Charles Dana. National Archives. LAS file. M-599, Reel 2.

180. Lee, E.G. General C.S.A. Diary of Edwin Gray Lee. Unpublished microfilm. James O. Hall Research Center. File copy.

181. Poore, B.P., ed. 1865. Conspiracy trial for the murder of the president, and the attempt to overthrow the government by the assassination of its principal officers. Testimony of John Holahan. J.E. Tilton and Company. Boston, Massachusetts. 1,577 pp.

182. Fisher, G.P. Hon. Presiding. 1867. Trial of John H. Surratt in the Criminal Court for the District of Columbia. Washington Government Printing Office. Testimony of David Barry. 678 pp.

183. Ibid.

184. Ibid.

185. Chaconas, J.L. 1988. Confession of George A. Atzerodt, published in Baltimore American newspaper January 18, 1869. Surratt Courier. A Publication of the Surratt Society & The Maryland-National Capitol Park & Planning Commission.

186. Fisher, G.P. Hon. Presiding. 1867. Trial of John H. Surratt in the Criminal Court for the District of Columbia. Washington Government Printing Office. Pierrepont submission of evidence. 678 pp.

187. Oldroyd, O. H. 1901.

188. Hall, J. O. 1982.

189. Fisher, G.P. Hon. Presiding. 1867. Testimony of David Barry.

190. Fisher, G.P. Hon. Presiding. 1867. Trial of John H. Surratt in the Criminal Court for the District of Columbia. Washington Government Printing Office. Testimony of J. A. McMillan. 678 pp.

191. Ibid.

192. Fisher, G.P. Hon. Presiding. 1867. Trial of John H. Surratt in the Criminal Court for the District of Columbia. Washington Government Printing Office. Testimony of Tinsley. 678 pp.

193. Jones, J.B. 1866. A Rebel War Clerks Diary. J.B. Lippincott & Co. Philadelphia, Pennsylvania. 482 pp.

194. Ibid.

195. Tidwell, W.A., J.O. Hall, and D.W. Gaddy. 1988. Come Retribution. The University Press of Mississippi. Jackson, Mississippi. 510 pp.

196. Poore, B.P., ed. 1865. Conspiracy trial for the murder of the president, and the attempt to overthrow the government by the assassination of its principal officers. Testimony of Louis Weichmann. J.E. Tilton and Company. Boston, Massachusetts. 1,577 pp.

197. Fisher, G.P. Hon. Presiding. 1867. Testimony of Tinsley.

198. Wheless, J.F. 1882. Letter regarding movement of Confederate States Treasure. Southern Historical Society Papers.

199. Poore, B.P., ed. 1865. Testimony of Louis Weichmann.

200. Surratt, J.H. 1870. Lecture at Rockville, Maryland. Transcript carried in December 7, 1870 edition of the Evening Star newspaper, Washington, D.C.

201. St. Lawrence Hall Register. 1864-65. Unpublished microfilm. James O. Hall Research Center. Maryland-National Capitol Park and Planning Commission. File copy.

202. Lee, E.G. General C.S.A. Diary of Edwin Gray Lee.

203. Ibid.

204. Poore, B.P., ed. 1865. Conspiracy trial for the murder of the president, and the attempt to overthrow the government by the assassination of its principal officers. Testimony of Robert Campbell. J.E. Tilton and Company. Boston, Massachusetts. 1,577 pp.

One block over, one block down from Mrs. Surratt's boarding house, Howard's stables were convenient for John Surratt to keep horses and rent rigs. Library of Congress, LC-DIG-cwpb-04203.

John Surratt, Mary Surratt and Nettie Slater stopped at Lloyd's tavern in Surrattsville, Maryland the morning of March 24 looking for Gus Howell who was to escort Nettie to Richmond. Photograph by author. Courtesy of Surratt House Museum/ MNCPPC.

CHAPTER TEN

Change of Plans

April 10–14, 1865

April 10, 1865 was a Monday in Washington and John Wilkes Booth was back home practicing with his favorite pistol: a small, easily concealed weapon known as a Derringer. It was the weapon of choice for gamblers and gentlemen. Booth fancied himself as both. The exercise was as much about settling his mind on a course of action as it was about perfecting his aim—a mental dress rehearsal each time he pulled the trigger. He had talked about killing Lincoln before.

"What an excellent chance I had, if I wished, to kill the President on inauguration day … I was as close to him nearly as I am to you,"[205] he had told a fellow actor and friend. Also, during a March meeting with fellow conspirators at Gautier's restaurant, Booth had to beat back a mutiny when he implied that killing Lincoln might be better than kidnapping him.[206]

Now his mind was made up, and it no longer mattered what the agents in Montreal, New York or Richmond thought. Booth convinced himself that assassinating Lincoln would save the failing Confederacy, or at least be just vengeance for the tyrant who started it all. More important, Booth—ever the narcissist—could claim all the glory for saving the South. Booth believed that no one could deliver the prize as effectively as he could. Lincoln loved the theatre, and Booth knew the venues well. No matter which show Lincoln chose, Booth planned to be there with pistol in hand.

On April 12, John Surratt, who was in Montreal, read a telegram from Booth calling for him to return immediately to Washington because the plan had changed.[207] Booth had no difficulty reaching Surratt at St. Lawrence Hall knowing that he could be back in Washington in a day and a half, maybe as early as noon on Good Friday, April 14.

Surratt knew that the fall of Richmond meant the kidnapping was out of the question. There was no Confederate government there to receive Lincoln. Surratt had also made a commitment to secret service chief Edwin G. Lee that he would go to Elmira, New York, to lay plans for freeing thousands of imprisoned Confederate soldiers there. This assignment would take him a week to complete before he could meet Booth in Washington. This time Booth would have to wait.

Meanwhile, Booth seethed in thoughts of Lincoln. He could not tolerate another Lincoln speech or his celebratory taunts or what Booth considered the president's petty military dictates. Booth felt as if he no longer had a country and fumed because Christian ministers who once prayed in earnest for Jeff Davis were now commanded to pray for Abe Lincoln.

On April 14, Booth was checking his mail, which he routinely had sent to Ford's Theatre as he had no permanent address in Washington. This morning on the steps in front of the theatre, he heard that Lincoln planned to attend the play at Ford's that night. Booth decided then and there it would be the night that he would take center stage, eliminate the tyrant and reap the glory.

Michael O'Laughlen was in Baltimore and reluctant to participate further in plotting against Lincoln. Fellow conspirator Samuel Arnold had left Baltimore on April 1 for his new job in Fortress Monroe, Virginia. Although Arnold knew that Booth had his letter about the plot that he had signed "Sam," he could not return to Washington from Fortress Monroe in time. But Booth could count on Mrs. Surratt to get Weichmann to help her retrieve the carbines and other gear from Lloyd's Tavern. Booth went to see her at the boarding house and they decided that Weichmann would drive the carriage to Surrattsville, and that she would keep him beyond ear-shot of her conversation with John Lloyd.

Booth also asked Herold and Atzerodt to meet that day with him in Powell's room at the Herndon House. He told them the kidnapping was off. Instead, he said, at 10:15 that night they would assassinate President Lincoln, Vice President Johnson and Secretary of State Seward.

Atzerodt immediately said he wanted no part in the murders.[208] Booth anticipated this and warned him he had better get his horse and be ready to go that night. The horse was a big problem for poor Atzerodt, and he knew it. Booth had not-so-generously allowed him to ride the horse all over town for two months. Atzerodt would be as good as caught if he didn't flee to Virginia with the others after the murders. So, reluctantly, he agreed to the change of plans.

Compromising co-conspirators had been effective for Booth, but Atzerodt had neither the skills nor personality for pulling off a murder. Springing the trap assured George Atzerodt's presence in Washington at Vice President Johnson's Kirkwood Hotel room on the night of April 14. It did not assure his effectiveness as an assassin.

Thus, Booth's escape plan was fatally flawed. The murders were to occur at 10:15 that night, and immediately afterward, Booth and the others had to quickly get out of Washington and across the Potomac River during the height of confusion in the city. But the crossing depended on Atzerodt retrieving the rowboat from where he had hidden it on the Potomac and rowing everyone across the river to the safety of Virginia.

Booth informed the others that he would assassinate President Lincoln at Ford's Theatre, and that Powell's assignment was to kill Secretary of State Seward, who was in his bed at home convalescing from injuries received in a recent carriage accident. Powell was strong and combat experienced, but he did not know his way around Washington. So, Herold's job was to escort Powell to Seward's house, hold his horse, then lead him out of the city after the deed was done. Powell was to get inside the house by faking a delivery of pharmaceuticals to the ailing secretary, then walk into the bedroom and shoot Seward.

Atzerodt's assignment was much simpler. He was to go to Vice President's room in the Kirkwood Hotel, which was unguarded, knock on the door and shoot Andrew Johnson point blank as he opened it.

Booth said he would use his Derringer and the others must carry revolvers. Misfires were possible, so each man must also carry a knife. Since Booth had not heard back from Surratt, Secretary of War Stanton would be spared, he said.

Atzerodt's and Powell's attacks were timed to occur as Booth slipped into the president's box at Ford's Theatre, removed his pistol from his pocket and shot Lincoln in the back of his head. Booth knew the play "Our American Cousin" by heart, and that only one actor would be on the stage when he pulled the trigger. Booth would then leap down from the box onto the stage, declare that the tyrant is dead and exit through a rear door where his horse would be outside waiting.

That night, the president and Mrs. Lincoln, followed by their guests, Major Rathbone and Clara Harris, arrived late at Ford's Theatre and were seated after the orchestra played "Hail to the Chief." Soon after 10 p.m. Booth was just outside the president's box and waiting for his cue from the only actor onstage: "You sockdologizing old man trap!" the actor said.

Meanwhile, Powell, with his back to Lafayette Square, was greeted at Seward's front door by house servant William Bell. Powell said he had medicine for the secretary that must delivered personally. But Bell said he would deliver it instead, so Powell shoved Bell aside and entered the house.

Frederick Seward, the secretary's son, met Powell at the top of the stairs, peeked into his father's room and denied entrance, saying his father was asleep. Powell feigned a retreat down the stairs then pulled out his pistol and tried to shoot Frederick, but the revolver misfired. Powell slammed the gun against Frederick's head repeatedly, knocking him senseless and breaking the pistol in the process. Powell pulled out his knife, forced his way past a guard as well as Seward's daughter Fanny, then slashed and stabbed the secretary repeatedly at his throat. Blood spewed amidst the screams, and in the dark room Powell was sure Seward was either dead or soon would be. Powell dashed out of the room, ran down the stairs and out the front door. Bell was out the door ahead of him screaming bloody murder and going for help.

Davy Herold was mounted and waiting outside when he heard the sounds of mayhem inside the house. Knowing something had gone wrong, he lost his nerve and galloped away before Powell could get out the door. Powell's mount was still there, but he did not know how to navigate Washington's confusing streets.

Meanwhile, Booth had slipped into the box, held his pistol to the back of Lincoln's head and fired. The bullet entered behind the president's left ear, crossed his brain diagonally and lodged above his right eye. With a bigger gun, death would surely have been instantaneous. Instead, the damage to Lincoln's brain was lethal but slow.

Booth used his knife to slash his way past Major Rathbone and jumped from the president's box for the stage below. He had performed stage leaps of equal heights before. But this time one of his boots snagged on a U.S. flag that had been draped on the rail of the box. Booth landed awkwardly on the stage and broke a leg. "*Sic semper tyrannis*," the actor yelled, limped off the stage, exited the theatre, mounted his waiting horse and rode out of town.

The moon was above the horizon[209] that night and defused light pierced the slight cloud cover as it illuminated Booth's way. Davy Herold was not far behind while Powell found a place to hide in a cemetery in Washington. He would show up three days later at Mary Surratt's boarding house.

The manhunt began before Lincoln died the next morning. It was obvious that the attacks were not coincidental, and everyone knew Lincoln's assassin was the famous actor John Wilkes Booth. Identifying Booth's fellow conspirators would take a little more time.

Literature Cited – Chapter Ten

205. Poore, B.P., ed. 1865. Conspiracy trial for the murder of the president, and the attempt to overthrow the government by the assassination of its principal officers. Testimony of Samuel Knapp Chester. J.E. Tilton and Company. Boston, Massachusetts. 1,577 pp.

206. Surratt, J.H. 1870. Lecture at Rockville, Maryland. Transcript carried in December 7, 1870 edition of the Evening Star newspaper, Washington, D.C.

207. Fisher, G. P. Hon. Presiding. 1867. Trial of John H. Surratt in the Criminal Court for the District of Columbia. Washington Government Printing Office. Vol. 1. Testimony of J. A. McMillan. 678 pp.

208. Chaconas, J.L. 1988. Confession of George A. Atzerodt, Published in Baltimore American on January 18, 1869. Surratt Courier. A Publication of the Surratt Society & The Maryland-National Capitol Park & Planning Commission.

209. Fisher, G. P. Hon. Presiding. 1867. Trial of John H. Surratt in the Criminal Court for the District of Columbia. Washington Government Printing Office. Vol. 1. Testimony of A. R. Eastman. 678 pp.

After he fired the fatal shot, John Wilkes Booth leaped from the president's box snagging his foot on the flag which resulted in the off-balanced landing that broke his leg. Days after the murder the flag remained—pulled slightly out of place by the assassin's foot. Library of Congress LC - B811 - 3403B.

CHAPTER ELEVEN

Elmira, New York

APRIL 7–19, 1865

WITH THE ARRIVAL of April, victory was still possible for the Army of Northern Virginia if it could reach North Carolina intact.[210] But by April 7, Robert E. Lee's army was reeling with extreme hunger, exhaustion from a forced march and the bloodletting on the banks of Sailor's Creek. There, at that unlikely place, Lee lost one-quarter of his remaining soldiers, and his retreat had degenerated into an attempt to survive to fight another day. His need for reinforcements was more acute than ever.

In Montreal, Confederate secret service chief Edwin G. Lee was working on a plan to free Confederate prisoners and reinforce the Army of Northern Virginia. John Surratt was in Montreal after delivering Secretary Benjamin's dispatches, which further directed Jacob Thompson in dispersal of Confederate funds.[211] Lee fully expected that Surratt would help if asked.

On April 7, with the understanding that five days earlier the Army of Northern Virginia had withdrawn from the trenches at Petersburg and that Richmond had fallen, Surratt realized there was little need now for his skills as a courier because the Confederate government had evacuated the capital.

He also knew that returning home to Washington was too risky because federal detectives would surely be there looking for him.

Back in central Virginia, the race west between the two armies was to be determined by who reached and controlled the railroad at Appomattox Station and west of Sailor's Creek. Union cavalry under George Armstrong Custer got there first and Lee was trapped. His army was grossly outmatched. He could stand, fight and be annihilated or he could surrender. He chose the latter. On April 9, 1865, telegraph lines hummed with the news of Lee's surrender, which soon reached the Confederates in Canada.

On April 10 a dejected John Surratt bought a train ticket for New York City, where he hoped to reunite with the lovely Nettie Slater. But later that day, Edwin G. Lee asked him to reconnoiter the prisoner-of-war camp in the southern part of New York State at Elmira where more than 5,000 Confederate soldiers were being held. The younger Lee still wanted to free the prisoners of war there. Confederate Gen. Joseph E. Johnston still commanded almost 90,000 Rebels who were scattered across several states—many of them in North Carolina—and Edwin Lee wanted to provide Johnston with the veteran reinforcements originally intended to support his famous cousin. Surratt—again inspired by hope for the cause that he found in Edwin G. Lee—accepted the assignment and set aside his trip to New York City.

First, Surratt needed a disguise to slip past federal detectives who could be anywhere from Montreal to Elmira and points in between. He called on a trusted Montreal tailor who fitted him with a Garibaldi jacket, a classic Canadian style unlike frock coats commonly worn in the United States. He left Montreal pretending to be Canadian who had little regard for Americans—an attitude that required no acting on his part.

Surratt arrived in Elmira on April 12, checked into a hotel and worked quickly gathering intelligence about the prison. This included the number of guards on duty; their hours and locations; the facility's points of ingress and egress; an accurate number of prisoners and their fighting capabilities; prison sketches and so on. Once freed, the men would need arms, ammunition, rations and a way to get down to North Carolina quickly and re-join the Confederate Army. In short, this mission required significant money.

Previously, Edwin G. Lee had asked Commissioner Thompson, who still controlled the Confederate purse there, for money to fund his plan to free the prisoners and reinforce the Army of Northern Virginia. But Thompson, whose primary focus was on himself, had some financial calculating to do before he gave away any more money.

April 9 was the day that news of Robert E. Lee's surrender reached Canada, and it was also the day Commissioner Thompson responded to Edwin G. Lee's request for money:

> *"Last evening I estimated that I would return $30,000 until you could hear from Mr. Benjamin. On second thought, however, I am unwilling to consent to this arrangement because it will hamper my movements and might prevent me from availing myself of a favorable opportunity of returning home—in other words, when I leave here I intend to be a free man."*[212]

Thompson opted for wealth as well as freedom, and thus pulled off a perfect crime: He had stolen a small fortune, almost half of the nation's remaining wealth, from the failed Confederacy, and as much as admitted this in writing to Edwin Lee. What he did not say was that on April 6—the same day Surratt delivered Secretary Benjamin's dispatch to Montreal—he withdrew $180,000 from the Confederate account, reducing it to his personal possession.

On April 10, Edwin G. Lee wrote a letter to his mother expressing hope that, despite the fall of Richmond and the surrender at Appomattox Courthouse, the Confederacy could survive. But, as he expressed to his mother, he was one of the few still in Canada who believed it. Jacob Thompson certainly did not. On April 11, Thompson withdrew almost all of the remaining funds from the Bank of Ontario, leaving a balance of only $1,766.23. Apparently, he wanted additional cash for his flight from Montreal to Halifax, Nova Scotia, and on to Europe.

Early on April 12, John Surratt wrote a letter to his mother, which he signed using his alias, "John Harrison," mailed it from the St. Lawrence Hall post office and left for Elmira, where he checked into the Brainard House.

He later scouted the prison, compiled his notes and made sketches of the facility. But he wasn't the only Surratt working on behalf of the crumbling Confederacy this holy week. And, John Surratt no longer controlled just how much his mother knew, and did, within the conspiracy.

Also on Wednesday, April 12, while John Surratt was riding the train to Elmira, Mary Surratt met with Richard Smoot when he stopped by the boarding house to get his final payment of $250 for sale of the boat[213] in which the conspirators planned to take Lincoln across the Potomac into Virginia. Mrs. Surratt asked Smoot if the boat was still in place because it would be used very soon. He said it was, and she assured him he would get the money within a few days of the crossing.

Since April 4, when Mary Surratt last saw or communicated with her son, she had met with Booth twice. For one of those meetings, she had instructed Weichmann to go to the National Hotel, contact Booth and ask him to call on her. After Booth arrived at the boarding house, he and Mary talked at the top of the stairs beyond earshot of any boarding house resident. She met with Booth again on Good Friday. And on that day, while her son John was busy in Elmira, New York, Mary Surratt went to Lloyd's Tavern in Surrattsville and told Lloyd to have the rifles—the "shooting irons," as she referenced them—ready because special visitors would stop by that night and pick up the gear hidden there. And, she handed Booth's field glasses, wrapped in brown paper, to Lloyd to supplement the equipment that he was to have ready.

Mary Surratt obviously was aware of the existence of Smoot's boat that Booth, agent Thomas Harbin and her son intended to use for the kidnapping. She knew that payment was due on the boat once the crossing was made, not before. She obviously was aware of the Spencer rifles cached on her property leased by John Lloyd. She also knew Booth sold the carriage in which the kidnapped president was to ride while being whisked out of Washington to the boat in southern Maryland.[214] She learned it when Weichmann went to Booth to borrow the carriage for a trip to Surrattsville and Booth said that he sold it. Booth then gave Weichmann money to rent one instead.

In other words, Mrs. Surratt knew then that no means existed to get Lincoln to the boat, but that Booth still planned to use it to cross the river. She knew that the Confederate government had abandoned Richmond and the Army of Northern Virginia had surrendered at Appomattox Courthouse, leaving no one to receive Lincoln. Obviously on the morning of April 14—Good Friday—Mary Surratt was aware that Booth had changed the kidnapping plan. She did not miss the point that violence was anticipated, hence having the "shooting irons" ready. And, she understood that whatever was about to happen, it would occur on April 14. John Surratt had no idea that his mother knew all this and more.

John Surratt, still pretending to be a brash Canadian, was up early and shopping for shirts Saturday morning, April 15, in Elmira, New York, when store clerk John Cass told him an assassin had shot Lincoln. On hearing this, Surratt did not conceal his approval. Cass was offended but dismissed the ill-mannered response as peculiar to a Canadian with little regard for Americans. Besides, he didn't want to lose a sale.

Soon afterward, Surratt heard that an actor shot Lincoln while he and Mrs. Lincoln were watching a play from the president's box in Ford's Theatre. Surratt hurried back to his hotel, packed his things and took the train to Canadaigua, New York. He knew he was a marked man.

Unfortunately for Surratt, trains did not run on Easter. Stuck and alone in Canadaigua on Easter Sunday morning, he went to Catholic mass before returning to his room at the Webster House, where he had registered as "J. Harrison."[215] In the hectic aftermath of Lincoln being shot and the bloody assault on Secretary of State Seward, newspaper reports included inaccuracies about the events. Some of it was bad reporting; other stories were based on falsehoods and misunderstandings leaked by government agents working with the U.S. Department of War. One fake news story jarred the not-easily-rattled Surratt. A New York newspaper identified the man who tried to kill Seward as John H. Surratt.[216]

Mrs. Slater was also on the move. She left New York City the day after Easter to rendezvous with Surratt. They last saw each other on April 5 when they were on the train from Washington to Canada via Baltimore and New York City. She got off in New York, where her mother and sister lived. Surratt stayed on the train to Montreal carrying the last dispatches ever to be delivered from Richmond to Confederate Canada.

From Canadaigua, Surratt could have taken a train west to Niagara Falls and crossed into Canada. That was the safest route where most of his trip to Montreal would have been north of Lake Ontario fully within the security of Canada. But Nettie Slater was to his east fleeing the United States from New York City toward St. Albans, Vt., then on to Montreal. Surratt wanted to see Nettie as much as she wanted to see him, so he chose to travel east to rendezvous with her near Albany, perhaps as far north as Whitehall, New York. The couple arrived together in Burlington, Vermont, traveling there by steamboat from Whitehall just before midnight April 17.[217] All of this Surratt and Slater could have coordinated by telegram. If not, the two had pre-arranged a response to disaster. Either way, they found each other. Then in Burlington, they were joined by Confederate agent Stephen Cameron.

They disguised themselves as poor, unkempt and men. Mrs. Slater, of course, was the smallest of the three, and she spoke to no one.[218] Either Cameron or Surratt was always positioned to protect Mrs. Slater from any curious innocent bystander. They spent the night at the train depot and left on the morning train to St. Albans. As expected, federal detectives were there looking for spies.

Surratt lit a cigar and left the others in search of food as well as the latest news about the assassination. He was not afraid to talk to strangers and casually read a newspaper that listed the names of the known conspirators. A bank clerk noticed him, was suspicious and followed him back to the depot. The clerk also made a mental note of a very short man who was with Surratt. The clerk's story was one of thousands of leads reported to authorities that day—although the majority were in Washington.

Also on April 17, U.S. detectives arrested Samuel Arnold in Fort Monroe, Virginia, and Mary Surratt that evening at her boarding house. Arnold gave investigators a detailed written statement leaving no doubt that John Surratt was Booth's chief co-conspirator. War Department Secretary Stanton and his detectives were convinced by then that multiple assassinations were the conspirators' goal from the start. Arnold's statement cast doubt on some of their assumptions. But they were certain that the chief co-conspirator John Surratt had been in Washington when Seward was attacked in his bed, and when Booth shot Lincoln, leaped onto the stage at Ford's Theatre then fled.

Maj. H.W. Smith—the same man who had questioned a surly Lewis

Powell following the servant girl incident in Baltimore early in the previous March—questioned Mrs. Surratt. She was evasive but yielded valuable information during the contentious process. Maj. Smith argued with Mrs. Surratt about her son's whereabouts, saying, "No man on the round earth believes he went to Canada." But Mrs. Surratt said, "I believe it." To which Smith responded, "No one can believe it, they would just as soon believe that a bird could fly if we cut off its wings."

As the interview continued, Mrs. Surratt noted she was a respected citizen of Washington and a responsible mother saying, "I assure you on the honor of a lady that I would not tell an untruth." Major Smith responded, "I assure you on the honor of a gentlemen, I shall get this information from you."[219]

Smith asked about the April 12 letter that Surratt sent his mother from Montreal, and which Weichmann told authorities he had seen. Was the letter misinformation intended to fool detectives about John's whereabouts? The detectives thought so. They speculated that Surratt left Montreal on April 12 and arrived in Washington in time for the April 14 assaults. They were confident they could catch him before made it back to Canada or nab him soon afterward in Montreal. But Surratt actually left Montreal on the morning of April 12 and went to Elmira, New York, and stayed there until April 15.

In an unfortunate coincidence for Lewis Powell, he arrived at the H Street boarding house late on April 17 when Major Smith and other Army officers were there to arrest Mary Surratt. Powell said he had come to dig drainage ditches on the property at the request Mrs. Surratt. But she said she had not hired him to do anything. Powell was not dressed like ditch digger, and the authorities noticed that his hands were not callused. He also wore an odd-looking hat that had been fashioned from a torn shirt sleeve. Powell was arrested along with Mrs. Surratt, but he offered no significant new information about the conspiracy.

The next afternoon, on April 18, Weichmann and Holohan prepared to leave Washington for Montreal along with detectives McDevitt, Bigley and Neese. Their assignment: Find John Surratt. Holohan packed among other items a shirt and handkerchiefs, which were among recently cleaned laundry left on his bed. But they did not belong to Holohan. At a corner of each handkerchief was embroidered "John H. Surratt No. 2." Weichmann and

Holohan left Washington with the detectives at 3 p.m. Tuesday and arrived on Wednesday morning April 19 in New York City. It was not clear if they went voluntarily, though Weichmann would later claim he did so.

On the evening of April 19, Weichmann, Holohan, McDevitt, Bigley and Neese arrived at St. Albans and registered using aliases at the American Hotel. They had just missed Surratt, Mrs. Slater and Cameron, who safely made it to Montreal the day before.

Conspirator Samuel Arnold's questioning by federal authorities was different from that of Mrs. Surratt. Arnold wrote out his statement before investigators began the interrogation. He was articulate and intelligent, impressing investigator William McPhail, and gave names, locations, a chronology and other details. His animosity toward Booth was obvious.

"Met him (Booth) the next day; went to breakfast together. He was pressed with business with a man unknown (to me), and then only by name, John Surratt,"[220] according to Arnold's written statement. That, of course was true, as was the fact that Surratt was Booth's co-conspirator. But Mary Surratt had not lied about her son being in Canada. John Surratt was not in Washington the night Lincoln was shot.

Did Mrs. Slater accompany Surratt to Elmira to reconnoiter the prison? Some historians think she did. This conclusion is based on the facts that "John Harrison," "A. Reynaud" and "T.F. Hendrickson" (aka, John Surratt, Mrs. Slater and Stephen Cameron) had arrived together on April 18 at 12:30 p.m. in Montreal four days after Lincoln's assassination and registered at St. Lawrence Hall.

Mrs. Slater clearly was with Surratt on the morning of April 4 when they left Washington via New York City for Montreal. It makes sense she was with him on April 6 upon arrival in Montreal. It would follow then that she traveled with him to Elmira and returned through Canadaigua back to Montreal on April 18. But why would two seasoned spies increase their risk for arrest by spending any more time than necessary in the United States? They could have made it into Canada early on the morning of April 17 via Niagara Falls.

Also notable is that Mrs. Slater was not registered at St. Lawrence Hall from April 6-12. Surratt was alone when he got there from Richmond. Was she staying elsewhere in the city? Not likely. Always before when in Montreal, she stayed at St. Lawrence Hall. No diary notes, hotel registries or witnesses placed her anywhere else in Montreal that week either. In addition, there was no evidence that she was in Elmira and Canadaigua when Surratt was in those places. No witnesses in John Surratt's trial testified that they saw anyone resembling Mrs. Slater there. The only name listed on registries in both towns was John Harrison. [221]

Her time in Richmond in late March and early April was unlike any other. She did not accompany Sgt. Brogden and Surratt to meet with Judah Benjamin even though she, not Surratt, brought the secretary dispatches from the Department of the North. Surratt only had filled in as her escort from Washington after the arrest of Gus Howell in Surrattsville. It's also noteworthy that Benjamin paid Surratt $200 in gold, twice the going rate for a spy mission. That only makes sense if the money was payment for both Surratt and Mrs. Slater.

Also interesting is the fact that Mrs. Slater left Richmond April 1 for the last time carrying two large travel trunks instead of one small one, as she had done so many times before. Lugging luggage on spy missions was difficult, especially when she had to get on and off and in and out of trains, carriages, ferries, rowboats and stagecoaches. She also had to haul luggage with her when she changed depots in Baltimore and New York City. That's why she typically carried only one small trunk while on assignment.

But on April 3 she carried two trunks when she got on the train to leave Washington, according to Atzerodt in his May confession to authorities. It appears she was permanently relocating to New York City to be near her mother and sister.

Meanwhile, Weichmann was scared. Was he a witness or a suspect? Secretary of War Edwin Stanton personally interviewed Weichmann as soon as he returned from Canada.[222] Another investigator, Col. B.F. Fisher, pressed him with pointed questions. Weichmann responded openly, trying to seem helpful. He told Fisher about a woman he thought was a Confederate spy, or at least a person of interest. He identified her as a Mrs. Slater, and described her as best he could.[223] The detectives surmised that Surratt might remain hidden in Canada. They were interested in this female companion who might be in Canada or hiding in the United States.

Literature Cited – Chapter Eleven

210. Jones, J.B. 1866. A Rebel War Clerk's Diary. J.B. Lippincott & Co. Philadelphia, Pennsylvania. 482 pp.

211. Surratt, J.H. 1870. Lecture at Rockville, Maryland. Transcript carried in December 7, 1870 edition of the Evening Star newspaper, Washington, D.C.

212. Levin, A.L. 1987. "This Awful Drama." Vantage Press, Inc. New York, New York. 248 pp.

213. Smoot, R.M. 1908. The Unwritten History of the Assassination of Abraham Lincoln. W. J. Coulter, Clinton, MS. Republished by Leopold Classic Library. 24 pp.

214. Fisher, G.P. Hon. Presiding. 1867. Trial of John H. Surratt in the Criminal Court for the District of Columbia. Washington Government Printing Office. Testimony of Louis J. Weichmann. 678 pp.

215. Fisher, G.P. Hon. Presiding. 1867. Trial of John H. Surratt in the Criminal Court for the District of Columbia. Washington Government Printing Office. Testimony of David Bates. 678 pp.

216. Surratt, J.H. 1870.

217. Ibid.

218. Baker, L.C., Col. USA. History of the United States Secret Service. 1867.

219. Surratt, M.E. 1865. Statement given to federal investigators April 17th. National Archives. LAS file. M-599, Reel 6.

220. Arnold, S.B. 1865. True copy of written statement given to federal investigators. National Archives. LAS file. M-619, Reel 458.

221. Fisher, G.P. Hon. Presiding. 1867. Trial of John H. Surratt in the Criminal Court for the District of Columbia. Washington Government Printing Office. Pierrepont submission of evidence. 678 pp.

222. Weichmann, L.J. 1975. A True History of the Assassination of Abraham Lincoln and the Conspiracy of 1865. Ed. Floyd E. Risvold. Alfred A. Knopf. New York. 492 pp.

223. Weichmann, L.J. 1865. Statement given to federal investigators May 25th. National Archives. LAS file. M – 599, Reel 3.

CHAPTER TWELVE

"Played for Mr. P"

APRIL 18–30, 1865

ON APRIL 18 at 12:30 p.m., "John Harrison," "Miss H.C. Slater" and "T.F. Hendrickson," all claiming to be from Connecticut, registered at St. Lawrence Hall in Montreal. Harrison was assigned to Room 121, Hendrickson got Room 113 and Miss Slater went to Room 114.[224] Like everywhere else, the topic of conversation was the assassination of President Lincoln. But St. Lawrence Hall no longer was safe refuge. There was too much attention focused here, too many detectives looking for John Wilkes Booth and John Harrison Surratt.

John Surratt had been widely reported as a conspirator, although his role as the man who attacked Secretary Seward was inaccurate. He slipped from his assigned room to Room 114. He was much safer there or across the hall until a safe house was located. All three agreed that they could not stay long at St. Lawrence Hall. This was reinforced by Edwin Gray Lee, who by then knew about Booth and Surratt, whom he referred to by the alias "Charlie Armstrong" or simply "C."[225] Lee had figured out by then that Booth changed the plan to multiple assassinations. Soon Lee would confirm much of what he knew when he read Samuel Arnold's confession in the daily newspaper:

"Most of his (Booth's) time was spent with him (Surratt). We were left entirely in the dark. Michael Loughlin (O'Laughlen) and myself rented a room in D Street 420 No. Obtained meals at Franklin House on the corner of 8th and D St. and there lived for nearly two months, seeing him (Booth) perhaps three or four times per week, and when seen always but a short time still pressing business always on hand viz. John Surratt.[226]

"The plan of escape was to place Mr. Lincoln in the buggy purchased for that purpose, cross Eastern Branch Bridge, Surratt and Atzerodt 'alias' Port Tobacco to pilot them to where a boat was concealed, turn horses loose, place the President in the boat and cross the Potomac to Virginia Shore and thence make our way to Richmond. Surratt knew the route and was to act as pilot."[227]

Lee, who was also a lawyer, understood the legal entanglements of conspiracy law. Culpability did not depend on participation in all phases or with all parties of the conspiracy. Booth's final stage appearance and his closing line *"Sic semper tyrannis!"* could render many Confederate leaders vulnerable to prosecution. Lee suspected that detectives would soon be in mass at St. Lawrence Hall. He also knew the fate of "Charlie Armstrong" if he were caught. Lee wondered who else might die at the end of a rope after being accused of participation in the Lincoln plot.

While at St. Lawrence Hall, Stephen Cameron and Mrs. Slater were seen walking around in the hotel, but Surratt stayed out of sight in the secure room. An inquisitive lady at teatime quipped to Cameron and Mrs. Slater about the other man who had been with them: "I expect you have got Booth in there."

"Perhaps so,"[228] she was told.

It wasn't long afterward that the trio left St. Lawrence Hall. Mrs. Slater simply disappeared. No one, then or later, reported her whereabouts. Cameron went to a house on Rue le Marion in northern Montreal.[229] He had many trusted contacts in the area, but in his journal, he simply noted, "Rue le Marion." Surratt told a hotel clerk that he had business in Quebec City, but remained in Montreal at the home of Confederate sympathizer John Porterfield.[230]

Confederate leadership in Canada was down to secret service chief Edwin G. Lee, Porterfield and Beverly Tucker. Lee still had the support of several loyal Confederate agents, for which he was grateful. For other Southerners still in Montreal, the transition from dangerous Rebels to powerless exiles was complete. And all wanted Surratt to leave Montreal as soon as possible. Porterfield provided temporary lodging for him while Cameron facilitated his move out of the city. Lee paid "Charlie Armstrong"—which he noted in his diary as being "For services to C, $40 expenses $100 for services."[231]

Cameron grew up as a Catholic before joining the Episcopal ministry. His ties to Catholic priests in Montreal and Quebec were strong. He wrote a letter to his friend, Father Boucher, about his need for a place to hide Surratt, and the priest agreed to help.

Weichmann, Holohan and the federal detectives passed through Burlington, Vermont, and spent the night of April 19 in St. Albans. Holohan lost one of the handkerchiefs bearing Surratt's name at the depot.[232] Soon after it was found, U.S. authorities swarmed the place thinking Surratt had been there, which happened to be correct. Weichmann and the others arrived in Montreal on April 20 just after noon. They registered at the St. James Hotel and walked to St. Lawrence Hall.

Weichmann checked the St. Lawrence Hall register and saw that Surratt had signed in using his alias and told the detectives.[233] But the hotel clerk said "Harrison" had left for Quebec City. After searching the streets of Montreal, Weichmann, Holohan, McDevitt, Bigley and Neese headed to Quebec.

By that time, the U.S. government had published a wanted poster with actual photographs—not sketches—of Booth, Herold and Surratt. It was the first time photos were used on such posters, which also listed whopping awards for the men's capture: $50,000 for Booth and $25,000 each for the other two. Accompanying the photos and reward offers was a warning: Anyone found harboring or failing to report the men's whereabouts would be considered accomplices, and subject to a military trial and the death penalty. Secretary of War Stanton had already determined that the trials would be handled by the military and those who were found guilty faced the death penalty.

The Confederates in Canada normally paid little notice to such threats, but with the fall of Richmond, things had changed significantly. Surratt was hiding inside Porterfield's house even though the place was under surveillance. In addition, both Dr. James Merritt, a physician from New York who spied on Confederates in Canada, and double-agent Sanford Conover had seen Surratt and Porterfield out on the street.[234] It would prove difficult to know with certainty what these two men really witnessed as both were gifted, self-aggrandizing liars.[235] U.S. detectives did not have authority to arrest Surratt at Porterfield's house, but it was only a matter of time before they could get Canadian police involved.

Agent Cameron quickly developed a plan to move Surratt to a safer hideout. Both Surratt and Cameron were tall and lean, and in low light closely resembled each other. It was after dark on April 21 when Confederate agents arrived simultaneously in two carriages in front of Porterfield's house. Two men in similar attire and appearance emerged from the house. One man got into one carriage and the other boarded the other. The drivers left in opposite directions. Cameron's ruse worked. Detectives watching the house were confused. Which carriage should they follow? Should leave their post at all? That evening Cameron noted his success in his journal: "Played for Mr. P."[236]

The next day, Cameron had arranged for Joseph Du Tilly to take Surratt to the home of Father Boucher in St. Liboire, a town just west of Quebec City. The letter that Cameron sent to the priest had paid off. On the last day of April, Cameron left for Quebec, and from there he continued to work on behalf of what was left of the Confederacy. He and secret service chief Edwin Lee had successfully kept "Charlie Armstrong" out of U.S. government hands.

Meanwhile, Mrs. Slater, eager to resume normal life in New York, had unfinished personal business to attend to. Her husband, Rowan Slater, had been in the Confederate Army for 10 months until the war was over. She had been a Confederate spy for five of them, and during that time much had changed. She did not want to be a farmer's wife living in North Carolina, and Nettie no longer loved Rowan Slater.

Literature Cited – Chapter 12

224. St. Lawrence Hall Register. 1864-65. Unpublished microfilm. James O. Hall Research Center. Maryland-National Capitol Park and Planning Commission. File copy.

225. Lee, E.G. General C.S.A. Diary of Edwin Gray Lee. Unpublished microfilm. James O. Hall Research Center. File copy.

226. Arnold, S.B. 1865. True copy of written statement given to federal investigators. National Archives. LAS file. M-619, Reel 458.

227. Ibid.

228. Surratt, J.H. 1870. Lecture at Rockville, Maryland. Transcript carried in December 7, 1870 edition of the Evening Star newspaper, Washington, D.C.

229. Cameron, S. F. (presumed author). Date unspecified. Untitled Manuscript, Notes for a "History of the Confederate Secret Service." Unpublished. James O. Hall Research Center file copy. 25 pp.

230. Surratt, J.H. 1870.

231. Lee, E.G. General C.S.A. Diary of Edwin Gray Lee.

232. Fisher, G.P. Hon. Presiding. 1867. Trial of John H. Surratt in the Criminal Court for the District of Columbia. Washington Government Printing Office. Testimony of Holohan. 678 pp.

233. Poore, B.P., ed. 1865. Conspiracy trial for the murder of the president, and the attempt to overthrow the government by the assassination of its principal officers. Testimony of L. J. Weichmann. J.E. Tilton and Company. Boston, Massachusetts. 1577 pp.

234. Poore, B.P., ed. 1865. Conspiracy trial for the murder of the president, and the attempt to overthrow the government by the assassination of its principal officers. Testimony of Sanford Conover. J.E. Tilton and Company. Boston, Massachusetts. 1577 pp.

235. Lovell (publisher). 1865. Testimony of Sanford Conover, Dr. J.B. Merritt, and Richard Montgomery before military court at Washington. The proofs disproving their statements and showing their perjuries. Toronto. 72 pp.

236. Cameron, S.F. (presumed author). Date unspecified.

April 18, 12:30 p.m., Stephen Cameron, Nettie Slater and John Harrison Surratt sign the register at St. Lawrence Hall using aliases. Photograph by author. Courtesy of Surratt House Museum/ MNCPPC.

"Let the stain of innocent blood be removed from the land ..." $25,000 reward is offered for John Surratt as he and the unknown Nettie Slater hide in Montreal. Library of Congress. hdl.loc.gov/loc.pnp/highsm.04756.

CHAPTER THIRTEEN

Person of Interest

APRIL 26–MAY 17, 1865

FEDERAL DETECTIVES—a mix of military officers, contractors and civilian lawmen—were pressured to arrest everyone involved in the assassination. At the same time, the increased amount of reward money offered by Secretary Stanton raised competition and reduced cooperation among them. Consequently, they often misused their authority and arrested suspects and witnesses on a hunch and held them indefinitely.

On April 26 in Baltimore, china shop owner Preston Parr was worried about his past associations and correspondence with collaborators involved in the Lincoln plot. Parr's extreme nervousness was justified, and in his mind, he was as good as caught. Three months previously, he had introduced Surratt to Powell, alias Lewis Paine, who was among the first suspects arrested. The two men had met at his china shop, and there were two female witnesses to that meeting. Also, Surratt had used the china shop to drop and retrieve many telegrams over many months.

Detectives opened their interrogation by showing Parr a copy of the March 14 telegram that he had received from Surratt. "Immediately telegraph if my friend is disengaged and can see me this evening in Washington."

Parr feigned cooperation, adding, "Let me be the first to say that disease of the stomach has somewhat affected my memory." Unimpressed with his spirit of cooperation and unsympathetic to any disease of the stomach, his interrogators applied more pressure. They showed Parr his telegram of the same date that he had wired back to Surratt. "She will be over in the six p.m. train."[237] His use of "she" in reference to Powell was to mislead others from thinking the message was in support of the Confederacy, but at this moment it was hard to explain.

"This (telegram) is another case," Parr responded. "At the same time, he (Surratt) met a girl at the store ... If my memory serves me, the lady was rather tall—I could not say. I should think not over 40. I should suppose 20—something in that neighborhood. As well as I can remember, she was rather slight. I am unable to say whether she was fair or dark complected (sic). Cannot tell how she was dressed—she was not dressed in mourning, but I took little notice. I should not think that she was dressed in colors. I should think not strictly dressed—not dressed strictly as a fine lady. Do not remember the name he called her by."[238]

To all of this rambling Parr added: "I am uncertain how often I have seen him. I should suppose three or four times—about three times ... I do not understand this telegram. I looked upon Mr. Surratt as a troublesome visitor ... I cannot explain the word 'she,' that woman may have gotten me to telegraph. I think I should remember it."[239]

Confederate spies often misused references to gender in telegrams, newspaper personals, letters and diaries. Examples include "Mrs. T" and "Mrs. Jacobs" for Jacob Thompson; "Mrs. Davis" for President Jefferson Davis; and in this case "she" for Lewis Powell. Federal detectives knew to look for it. They thought Preston Parr remembered it.

Despite of Parr's vagueness, his questioning yielded one key point: He confirmed that Surratt had come to his shop in the company of young lady who was slight of frame—as well as he could remember.

Meanwhile William Bell, who met the attacker at the door of Secretary Seward's home the night of the assault, had positively identified Powell—not Surratt as previously reported in newspapers—as the attacker. Even so,

Surratt had remained the manhunt's primary target behind Booth, who was killed earlier that day. And Atzerodt, who was lodged in the old penitentiary at the Washington Arsenal, was talking. Although his statements were long, rambling and confusing, they increasingly detailed Surratt's involvement with a mysterious lady who used several aliases.

"Kate Thompson, alias Brown, came from Richmond with John Surratt about the time Richmond fell," Atzerodt told them. "She come previously with Gustavus Howell (now in the Old Capitol Prison). Kate Thompson stopped at Mrs. Surratt's, and also at the National and Rinnel hotels. This woman was about 21 years of age, spruce, neat, medium size, black eyes and with a fair complexion. She had a sister in New York who, it is said, was a widow."[240]

Later he added: "Mrs. Surratt, Mrs. Slater, Major Banon and John Surratt left Washington together; got horses at Howard's (stable). Mrs. S. (Surratt) stopped at Surrattsville. John Surratt and Mrs. Slater crossed (the Potomac River), and Banon and Mrs. Surratt came back (to Washington)."[241] Then he said: "Mrs. Slater went with Booth a good deal. She stopped at the National hotel."[242]

Atzerodt reiterated these observations when offering a separate, independent statement that also included: "Kate Thompson or Kate Brown, as she was known by both names, put up at the National & was well known at the Penn House. She knew all about the affair. Surratt went to Richmond with her last March & Gust. Howell made a trip with her to the same place. This woman is about 20 years of age, good looking & well dressed. Black hair & eyes, round face from South Carolina & a widow … Young Weightman (Weichmann) at Surratt's ought to know about this woman."[243]

Indeed, Louis Weichmann did know about Mrs. Slater. Mrs. Surratt had told him that the young woman was a blockade runner, that she spoke French, and she might claim French citizenship to avoid arrest. And Weichmann willingly shared the details that he knew during his interviews with Secretary of War Stanton and Col. B.F. Fisher.

"I think when Mrs. Slater ran the blockade must have been some time in the month of February, in the beginning of the month," Weichmann said. "She had her veil down, and I cannot describe her. She was short and thin. I never had a moment's conversation with her in my life; never saw her face; her veil was always worn. The longest she stayed at Mrs. Surratt's was one night, if I remember correctly."[244]

Later Weichmann added, "Surratt left the house with a woman named Slater on March 27. Came back on 2nd of April. He had nine or 11 pieces of gold."[245] And: "Mrs. Slater is a blockade runner. Learned from Mrs. Surratt that she and Surratt had gone to Richmond … Holohan has seen her at the (boarding) house twice. I saw her but once; always had her veil …"[246] Weichmann attempted to be honest, but he was not exact in reporting dates. Mrs. Slater and John Surratt actually had returned to Washington on April 3.

At that point the detectives knew that John Surratt had traveled with a woman, and multiple witnesses placed them together. But descriptions of her were vague. She appeared to be significantly involved, and perhaps Surratt was in hiding with her. If not, she might have known where he was. All they had to do was find her.

On May 10, the trial of conspirators began on the third floor of the Old Penitentiary, within the war-expanded grounds of the Washington arsenal. Proceedings were not encumbered by presumption of innocence of the accused. Secretary of War Stanton picked the nine-member military commission that served as the jury, and they were seated as directed by the U.S. assistant adjutant general.

The jurors included three major generals, four brigadier generals, one colonel and one lieutenant colonel. Major Gen. David Hunter was commission president.[247] All were loyal Stanton men who were told to establish the rules and conduct the proceedings to achieve swift "public justice."

Arraigned and sitting before this tribunal were eight suspects: Samuel Arnold, Dr. Samuel A. Mudd, Edman "Ned" Spangler, Michael O'Laughlen, George A. Atzerodt, Lewis Payne (Powell), David E. Herold and Mary E. Surratt.[248]

All were charged with "combining, confederating and conspiring, together with one John H. Surratt, John Wilkes Booth, Jefferson Davis, George N. Saunders, Beverly Tucker, Jacob Thompson, William C. Cleary, Clement C. Clay, George Harper, George Young and others unknown, to kill and murder, within the Military Department of Washington, and within the fortified and intrenched lines thereof, Abraham Lincoln, late, and at the time of said combining, confederating and conspiring, President of the United States of America ..."[249]

The government called numerous witnesses. Testimonies and cross examinations yielded damning evidence against those accused, including those whose were not prisoners at the bar, along with the condemnations of the eight who were. One of the unknowns was Nettie Slater, who had left Canada and returned to New York City. Surely she was nervous about the trial and followed the testimony closely as reported daily in New York newspapers, all the while continuing to wonder who might be watching her.

On May 13, the government's star witness, Louis J. Weichmann, took the stand. His words were especially damning to Mary Surratt and Dr. Mudd. He continued to testify on May 15, 18 and 19:

Question: "What knowledge do you have of John Surratt having gone to Richmond?"

Weichmann: "About the 17th of March, a woman by the name of Mrs. Slater came to the house and stopped there one night. This lady went to Canada and Richmond. On Saturday the 23rd of March, Mr. Surratt drove her into the country about eight o'clock in the morning ... He left in company of Mrs. Slater, and Mrs. Surratt was also in the buggy."

Question: "It was your understanding that John H. Surratt went to Richmond?"

Weichmann: "Yes, sir. On returning, Mrs. Surratt told me that he had gone to Richmond with Mrs. Slater. This Mrs. Slater, to the best of my knowledge, was to have met a man by the name of Howe there—a blockade runner. This Howe was captured on the 24th of March and could not take her back to Richmond. So, Surratt took her back."

Mary Surratt's attorney, Frederick Aiken, cross examined Weichmann. Aiken, a former Army captain wounded in the war—was now a young, inexperienced lawyer defending Mary in a death-penalty military tribunal. Thus, the rules of conduct regarding justice were established in a way that was neither balanced nor blind.

Aiken: "How did you learn anything with reference to the antecedents of Mrs. Slater?"

Weichmann: "It was told me by Mrs. Surratt herself."

Aiken: "What did Mrs. Surratt tell you?"

Weichmann: "Mrs. Surratt said that she came to the house in company of this man Howell; that she was a North Carolinian, I believe; and that she was a blockade runner or bearer of dispatches."

Aiken: "Did you have and conversation with her (Slater) yourself?"

Answer: "She drove up to the door in a buggy. The bell rang, and there was a young man in the buggy with her. Mrs. Surratt told me to go out and take her trunk. That is all the communication I had with her. She had a mask down—one of the short masks ladies wear. They call them masks, I believe. They are not veils.

Question: "What was it made of?

Answer: "Crepe. They do not cover the entire face. They come down to the chin."[250]

On May 27, Augustus Spencer Howell, who had been a Confederate agent, took the stand. Howell knew enough to seriously implicate Nettie Slater depending upon what he was asked and how cooperative he would be in answering.

Question: "Have you ever been to her (Mary Surratt's) home in this city?"

Howell: "Yes, I was there once."

Question: "At what time was that?"

Howell: "It was February last. I believe the 20th of February."

Question: "State to the court why you went there."

Howell: "I went there on a visit as much as anything else. I had no business there particularly, except that."

Question: "In February, who accompanied you to Richmond?"

Howell: "There were some half a dozen, I believe, that went to Richmond with me. Principally persons from the neighborhood in the county."

Question: "What was your business in December in going to Richmond?"

Howell: "Nothing. I had no particular business there at all, more to see some of my friends ..."

Question: "What was your business in February?"

Howell: "In February, I went down to see some of my friends. I had no particular business at all."

Question: "I wish to ask you whether or not your business substantially for the last year and a half—was going to and from Richmond?"

Howell: "No, sir. That was only because I chose to do it, that was all, not any business."

Question: When you went to Richmond in February, can you remember the names of the persons who accompanied you?

Howell: "There was a young man by the name of "Fow" who accompanied me. ("Fow" was Confederate agent James Fowle, who had accompanied Mrs. Slater on her first mission to Canada.)

Question: When you were at the Surratt house, did you ever meet a person there by the name of Mrs. Slater?"

Howell: "No sir: I never met her there."

Question: "Or a person that went by that name?"

Howell: "I never met her at Mrs. Surratt's."

Question: "Where did you meet her?"

Howell: "I met a lady by that name in Washington."

Question: "Where?"

Howell: "She came in front of Mrs. Surratt's house."

Question: "When?"

Howell: "That was in February."

Question: "Did she accompany you to Richmond?"

Howell: "Partly."

Question: "Where to?"

Howell: "We went to Virginia together."

Question: "Did she come back with you?"

Howell: "I happened in with her accidentally, and we came back together."[251]

Howell's testimony was effective. He managed to get Assistant Judge Advocate Burnett tied in knots simply trying to get his name right. Howell yielded only what he absolutely had to, and even then his answers were hazy. He covered for Mrs. Slater and Mrs. Surratt with outright lies and clever omissions of truth.

Question: Why did you not give (your name) when you were under oath?

Howell: "I do not know. I was not particular in the name. He asked what my name was, and I told him."

Question: "Is Spencer your name?"

Howell: "It is one of my names. It is not used generally, except sometimes by my friends."

Question: "Then did you give your correct name when you said it was 'Augustus Howell'?"

Howell: "Yes sir. That is my correct name."

Question: "Then is 'Augustus Spencer' your correct name?"

Howell: "A.S. Howell."

Question: "How long have you had the name Spencer?"

Howell: "For some time. I do not know how long."

Question: "Was it given to you in infancy?"

Howell: "Some of my friends used to call me that."

Question: "Were you named in infancy Augustus Spencer Howell?"

Howell: "I do not know."

Question: "Since how long have you had that name?"

Howell: "My friends generally call me that."

Question: "I am not asking you what your friends call you. You know your own name."

Howell: "That is my name. I have told you so."

Question: "Did you give the court the name of Augustus Spencer Howell?"

Howell: "I gave you the name A.S. Howell."

Question: "Is that all your name?"

Howell: "That is my name."

Question: "Or are those the initials of your name?"

Howell: "The initials, of course."[252]

Weichmann offered details that were problematic for Mrs. Slater. Howell did not.

Literature Cited – Chapter Thirteen

237. Parr, P. 1865. Statement given to federal investigators April 26th. National Archives. LAS file. M-599, Reel 5.

238. Ibid.

239. Ibid.

240. Chaconas, J.L. 1988. Statement of George A. Atzerodt to Prov. Mar. McPhail in Presence of John L. Smith on the Night of May 1 – 1865. Surratt Courier. A Publication of the Surratt Society & The Maryland-National Capitol Park & Planning Commission.

241. Ibid.

242. Ibid.

243. Ibid.

244. Weichmann, L.J. 1865. Statement given to federal investigators May 25th. National Archives. LAS file. M-599, Reel 3.

245. Ibid.

246. Ibid.

247. Poore, B.P., ed. 1865. Conspiracy trial for the murder of the president, and the attempt to overthrow the government by the assassination of its principal officers. Tribunal. J.E. Tilton and Company. Boston, Massachusetts. 1,577 pp.

248. Ibid, Arraignment.

249. Ibid, Charges.

250. Poore, B.P., ed. 1865. Conspiracy trial for the murder of the president, and the attempt to overthrow the government by the assassination of its principal officers. Testimony of Louis J. Weichmann. J.E. Tilton and Company. Boston, Massachusetts. 1,577 pp.

251. Poore, B.P., ed. 1865. Conspiracy trial for the murder of the president, and the attempt to overthrow the government by the assassination of its principal officers. Testimony of Gus Howell. J.E. Tilton and Company. Boston, Massachusetts. 1,577 pp.

252. Ibid

CHAPTER FOURTEEN

War of Words

May 5–August 25, 1865

IN LATE APRIL 1865 Secretary of War Stanton sent a dispatch to Gen. John Dix claiming that agents working with Confederate commissioners in Canada, as well as Confederate authorities in Richmond, organized Lincoln's assassination and were involved in carrying it out. His accusations, while unambiguous, were unsupported with proof. The opening strategy in the trial of conspirators was to prove this assertion and in effect convict the Confederacy and its leaders in Lincoln's murder and the bloody assault on Secretary Seward.

As April drew to a close, Edwin G. Lee—who remained in Canada—publicly criticized Stanton in a letter published in the *Montreal Gazette.* Lee said no one in Confederate government authorized Lincoln's assassination; that all were ignorant of the plot. He praised the character of Confederate President Davis and Secretary of State Benjamin while challenging that of the vengeful U.S. Secretary of War. Lee's qualifications in support of his claims were personal communications with Davis and Benjamin regarding conduct of the war. And Lee was not alone in denying Confederate government complicity.[253]

An editorial in the *Montreal Gazette* supported Lee and noted that Stanton's dispatch was extraordinary. The editorial accused Stanton of being the "medium of a disgraceful libel." Lee's article was reprinted in the *Baltimore Gazette* on May 5. An indignant Lew Wallace, major general of the United States Volunteers, telegraphed a proposal to Secretary Stanton in response to the publication of Lee's comments:

> *"Please read an article in the Baltimore Gazette of this a.m. signed Edwin G Lee, Brig. Genl. CSA, to the Editor of the Montreal Gazette. I consider the publication of said article an insult to you and the Government and justification to suppress the (Baltimore) journal unless you command to the contrary. Please reply so that I can act tonight."*[254]

Edwin G. Lee had chosen his words carefully. Note that he wrote about the assassination, omitting any reference to the proposed kidnapping. By the date of his published letter, it is inconceivable that he did not know about the kidnapping plot. Lee was truthful and likely accurate that Confederate leaders knew nothing of Booth's shift in objectives. But conspiracy law, then and now, would allow prosecutors to link the act of planning to kidnap Lincoln with that of committing his murder by deed. By law, it could be argued, all members of the kidnapping conspiracy did not have to be present when the plans changed, or even cognizant of the details, to be culpable for the assassination.

Further, it would be extremely difficult to separate Booth's and Surratt's conspiracy to kidnap Lincoln from that of Thomas Conrad's—both plans being practically identical and most likely of common origin. Confederate leaders could also be charged with organizing and approving what was known as the Blackburn Yellow Fever Plot against Lincoln from Montreal, and the Harney explosives plot against Lincoln from Richmond.

But Lee probably didn't know of the other conspiracies, and in fairness to Secretary Stanton, his words were in a dispatch to subordinates. They were not meant to be shared directly with the public.

However, the threat by Gen. Wallace to shut down the Baltimore newspaper for publishing Edwin Lee's letter was outside the finer points of conspiracy law as well as those of the U.S. Constitution. For years after the firing on Fort Sumter, the U.S. military had been closing down "disloyal" newspapers in both the United States and the Confederate States. His proposal was go to Baltimore under the cover of darkness and close down a newspaper for publishing an article that insulted the U.S. government and especially the U.S. Secretary of War.

Suppression of rights of American citizens to criticize their government would not have been a first for Gen. Wallace. A little more than two weeks earlier, he warned a clergyman in Baltimore about behavior in church:

> *"You will perceive the propriety of requiring members of your congregation, male and female, who may be so unfortunate as to have been sympathizers with the rebellion, not to bring their politics into church. ... I choose this method of respectfully warning you ... You know what I request, I have the power to enforce ...*
>
> *"If you feel that you cannot yourself comply with this fraternal solicitation or that you are unable to control evil-disposed members of your flock, I suggest that it is better, far better, in every respect, that you should close the doors of your church for a season at least."*[255]

Edwin G. Lee's letter was not the only one critical of U.S. authorities. On the same day, former Confederate agent Beverly Tucker, who was in hiding, asserted that whoever accused him of being involved in the assassination or any knowledge of the plot to capture Lincoln or Seward "blackened his soul with diabolic perjury."[256] His protest included denial of ever having heard of John Wilkes Booth before the assassination.[257] But this did not keep Tucker off the list of Confederates charged in absentia at the trial of conspirators.

Meanwhile, Mrs. Slater's husband Rowan—one of 45,000 Confederate soldiers captured soon after Robert E. Lee pulled out of Petersburg—was released after the surrender. Mrs. Slater was back in New York City by then and preparing to file for a divorce. So, Rowan Slater went to New York in search of his wife.

Divorce was a matter of record, and some newspapers published sensational details. Such was the case in New York State. For example, the divorce proceedings involving a woman named Mary Stevens Strong, who, after having three daughters with her husband, admitted she had committed adultery with her brother in-law, who had been living with them.[258] Nettie Slater certainly did not want such details of her divorce reported for all to see, especially considering her service to the Confederacy.

Rowan Slater arrived in New York City and tried to work things out with his wife, but he returned to North Carolina alone. Subsequently, on June 12, the *Hartford* (Connecticut) *Evening Press* published a story written by a correspondent in New Bern, N.C.:

> *"In the investigations concerning the assassination of the president frequent mention is made of a 'Mrs. Slater' said to be a French Woman or of French descent. If the reports of the natives here (New Bern) be true, Hartford has an interest in said investigation.*
>
> *"About the year 1858 or '59, a young lady lived in Hartford by the name of Gilbert, who came to North Carolina about 1859 or '60, and boarded in New Bern, at the house of Pennington, the editor of the Daily Progress. Said lady became acquainted with and married a dancing master by the name of R. Slater, who entered the rebel services when war came on. Those who belong here and who have been in the rebel service all say that the Mrs. Slater mentioned in the investigations at Washington is the identical lady above mentioned. That being generally conceded amongst her acquaintances here, if any of her friends have proof to the contrary, they had better produce it if they don't like the associations.*
>
> *"Said lady had two brothers who were among the first to volunteer in the rebel service, and assisted the traitors as part of the first garrison of Fort Macon, under rebel rule, and were as alert and zealous as true disciples. Although I have been told in Connecticut (by a lady of New Britain) that they wrote home that they were forced into rebel service against their will, I know it was a mistake.*
>
> *Yours, REBEL HATER."*[259]

On the same day, the following was published in the *Hartford Courant*:

> *"A correspondent of the Press, writing from New Bern, N.C., intimates that the 'Mrs. Slater' who has figured somewhat in the trial of the parties concerned in the assassination of the President, is a Hartford woman; that about the year 1858 or 1859 she went to New Bern and married Slater, who was a dancing master. Her maiden name was Gilbert. Does anyone here know of her?"*[260]

The *Courant* on June 13 printed the following:

> *"The woman "Mrs. Slater," who has figured in the assassination trial, and who, it has been suggested, formerly lived in Hartford, did reside here in 1858. She and her mother, a Mrs. Gilbert, rented a house on Windsor Street, of S.A. Ensign, Esq., and were professedly engaged in music teaching, though our informant does not know whether they had any pupils or not. Early in '59 the young woman went South, and, as stated by a correspondent of the Press, married a Mr. Slater, a dancing master in Newbern, N.C."*[261]

On June 16, the *Courant* ran another story:

> *"Mrs. Slater, who has appeared in the assassination trial, and who was spoken of in the Courant as having lived in Hartford, is well known here. She resided here with her parents for several years. Her father was Dr. Joe Gilbert, called a doctor because of his manufacture of pills. He was at one time a teacher of the French language at the High School. Her name was Sarah, and she enjoyed (?) a doubtful reputation during the latter days of her residence here. She removed to Hartford in 1858, and went South as has been stated."*[262]

Whether Mrs. Slater was aware of "Rebel Hater's" articles is not known. But she had lived in New Bern, N.C., and married local dance instructor Rowan Slater. It's likely that the newspaper articles in the Connecticut newspapers came to her attention in nearby New York. If so, Mrs. Slater surely was nervous. Would federal detectives read the *Courant* and make the connection? What would her family members in New York say if detectives asked about her? Should she return to the safety of Canada? There is strong evidence that indeed she did return to Canada, where she was reunited with John Surratt.

On July 6, 1865, at a little before noon, Major Gen. John Hartranft, commander of the U.S. Arsenal Military Prison, and Major Gen. Winfield Scott Hancock, his superior, delivered death warrants to four of the eight conspirators. They were to be hanged the following day. Workers immediately began building gallows on prison grounds, while the others accused in the conspiracy awaited news of their fates.

It was hot and muggy on the afternoon of July 7 in Washington when the four condemned conspirators climbed the stairs of the gallows to a platform where four chairs and four nooses awaited them. Mary Surratt had a difficult time reaching the platform. Once there, she sat in a chair facing her noose and positioned to the right of the unflinching Lewis Powell, who was still known by his alias Lewis Payne. When his hat inadvertently fell to the ground, it was returned to him. Powell responded with a thank you, adding "I shall not need it much longer." Mrs. Surratt and Powell would share the same trap door. She was nervous as she clung to the hope that President Andrew Johnson would grant her a last-minute pardon because she was a woman.

The prisoners were told to stand. Powell stood first and proclaimed that Mrs. Surratt was innocent, as he had done the previous day in a conversation with Gen. Hartranft. Powell had no reason to lie.

"Please don't let me fall," Mrs. Surratt said as she was told to stand.

Judge Joseph Holt, who presided over the trial, was aware of Powell's assertions of Mary Surratt's innocence, and had requested a written explanation of this from Father Jacob Walter, who was working on Mrs. Surratt's behalf. Earlier that day, Gen. Hartranft added a comment to Father Walter's response to the judge: "I believed Payne (Powell) had told the truth in this matter."[263]

Gen. Hartranft's comment drew immediate attention, and he was asked to clarify it. He said he merely accepted, as sincere, Powell's assertion that

Mrs. Surratt's was innocent of conspiracy to kill Lincoln, then squelched the notion that the trial was flawed. Hartranft personally did not conclude that Mary Surratt was innocent of conspiring to murder Lincoln.

Mrs. Surratt died that day along with the other three conspirators. Lewis Powell and Davy Herold were positioned on the gallows behind rather than under the crossbeam, which allowed them to swing grotesquely fore, aft while still alive after the drop, and each died hard and slowly. But Mrs. Surratt's neck snapped quickly, and she died immediately. Atzerodt's end also was quick. Justice was served; the message was delivered: There would be no tolerance of guerilla warfare or other acts of rebellion by anyone regardless of gender. Hanging the middle-aged woman drove home the point. Mrs. Mary Elizabeth Surratt was the first woman to be officially executed by the United States government.

While the sights, sounds and drama of the execution unfolded, those conspirators not sentenced to hang that day remained ignorant of their fates. But days later, Sam Arnold, Dr. Samuel Mudd and Michael O'Laughlen received life sentences. They were only one vote away (five instead of six guilty votes from the tribunal of nine) from also going to the gallows. Ned Spangler got a six-year sentence. The prisoners were transferred to Fort Jefferson in Florida's Dry Tortugas. O'Laughlen died of yellow fever there in September 1867. President Johnson pardoned Dr. Mudd in February 1869, and pardoned Arnold and Spangler a month later.

The news about Mrs. Surratt's hanging stunned Nettie Slater and the Confederate agents remaining in Canada. Nettie knew Mary Surratt, and that her son had tried to keep her out of the conspiracy. Nettie did not know Mary played an active role in Lincoln's assassination and Booth's subsequent attempt to escape into Virginia.

In Canada, John Surratt had been sick with malarial chills and fever on the day his mother died. He knew only what he was told by his protectors, and news of her pending execution was not included. Any attempt by him to help his mother—such as offering himself in exchange for her—would have endangered the others.

Weeks earlier he was warned to lay low: "Be under no apprehension as to any serious consequences. Remain perfectly quiet, as any action on your part would only tend to make matters worse. If you can be of any service to us, we will let you know; but keep quiet."[264]

He later blamed those who withheld information for his failure to help his mother.

Nettie Slater knew that John Surratt and his mother were very close, and the others feared he might try to save her if he understood her full measure of peril. Some thought she was merely bait to draw out her son from hiding. But there was no way for him to save her, and few people believed the government would actually execute a woman regardless of her crime. All the while, Secretary Stanton threatened to hang anyone hiding John Surratt or taking part in the conspiracy—Mrs. Slater included.

The following month, on August 7, Edwin G. Lee and a friend, Dan Lucas, boarded the steamer *Montreal* in the city of that name for a trip to Quebec. They needed a break and looked forward to seeing more of Canada. Lee also missed his wife, who had returned to the United States almost a month earlier. Lee watched parades in Quebec, attended theatrical performances and went fishing.[265] But there was another reason for the trip: Lee wanted to meet with John Surratt to discuss his situation.

In Quebec, Lee and Lucas met up with John Lovell, his wife and a woman named Miss Young of New York City. She had been staying with the Lovells for several days, completely trusted and exceptionally good looking. Two days later Surratt arrived in Quebec, having traveled 185 miles north from his hideout in St. Liboire. That evening he escorted Miss Young to the theatre. They enjoyed actor Charles Kean's performance as Shakespeare's Richard II. Members of their party also played cards, took walks and enjoyed fine dining at the posh Riverton Hotel, frequented by wealthy Brits.

Lee wrote in his journal that he enjoyed the change of scenery, as well as little things, including playing hands of the card game whist—which had four players, two partnerships—with friends. Surratt also enjoyed himself because he no longer sequestered in what amounted to house arrest, and now was in the company of the lovely Miss Young.

Still, Lee and the others had serious decisions to make: What should they do with Surratt? He couldn't hide in Canada for the rest of his life. Too risky. And what about Miss Young—who surely was Nettie Slater?

Lee and Surratt discussed John's future, which had to include his pending independence from Confederate support and what might be the best outcome for Nettie Slater. A Canadian identified only as Bouthiller, who knew his way around the countryside, would continue to help for now. Bouthiller had been helping Father Charles Boucher hide and care for Surratt in St. Liboire. Lee agreed to work out details of the pending move with Beverly Tucker and Stephen Cameron. The cost would be covered with cash from what little was left in the Confederate account.

On August 11 Lee noted in his journal: "Dined with Armstrong & Bouthiller." On August 12 he wrote: "Took walk with Armstrong and B."[266] He continued to refer to Surratt as "Charlie Armstrong," "Charlie," "C," or "Armstrong." He also referred to someone whose alias was "Young" as a pseudonym, sometimes writing "Miss Young" or "the Young." It was never proved beyond a doubt that "Miss Young" was Nettie Slater, but evidence strongly suggests so. She had an ongoing romantic relationship with Surratt, and he was devoted to her.[267]

Surratt had long been ill with *fevres tremblantes* to the point that Father Boucher feared he would die.[268] Surratt's contacts while in hiding included several men who visited with him, shared stories and generally enjoyed each other's company. On days when Surratt felt relatively good, he walked around outside. But he was not healthy enough and secure enough to meet and develop an amorous relationship with another woman.

It is interesting to note that Nettie Slater began her spy missions to help Lt. Bennett Young and other St. Albans raiders. Could this be why Lee referred to a "Miss Young" in Canada? Also, she was described and being young and pretty and from New York. She was also trusted by Lee with confidential information about John Surratt. The evidence strongly suggests that "Miss Young" and Mrs. Slater were one and the same.

On August 14 the Confederates left Quebec and everyone except Surratt returned to Montreal. But he soon rejoined them, perhaps because he wanted to be with his girlfriend. Neither of them could stay long in Canada, as noted by Lee in his journal:

"August 21. Raining nearly all day. Lucas didn't return from Chambly. Mr. Armstrong very devoted: made an opportunity for him in the library—and after his departure at 8 p.m., for Miss Hercazque & her beau on the front steps. Had a very confidential conversation with "The Young" after returning from theatre at 11 p.m."[269]

On August 25, Lee wrote: "Feeling pretty badly. Shopped a little & spent three hours on St. Cathn. Street. At night took Miss Emily to Mrs. Tiffin's little party. Dan didn't come in—too late of course. Armstrong arrived at 7 p.m. The Young left at 12 midnight."[270]

Little more of interest about the conspiracy was reported in the newspapers at that time, so Nettie Slater apparently returned to New York to settle the divorce with her estranged husband.

Literature Cited – Chapter 14

253. Tucker, B. 1865. Letter to editor. The *Alexandria Gazette.* May 5.

254. Wallace, L. 1865. Telegram to Secretary of War Stanton. Office U.S. Telegraph. National Archives. LAS file. M-473, Reel 118.

255. Wallace, L. 1865. Letter to Baltimore clergy. National Archives.

256. Tucker, B. 1865. Letter to editor. *Brooklyn Daily Sentinel.* May 5.

257. Tucker, B. 1865. Letter to editor. The *Alexandria Gazette.*

258. *The New York Times.* 1865. Divorce case Mary Stevens Strong. November 30, 1865 and December 1, 1865.

259. *Hartford Evening Press.* 1865. June 12. James O. Hall Research Center. Maryland-National Capitol Park and Planning Commission. File copy.

260. The *Courant.* 1865. June 12. James O. Hall Research Center. Maryland-National Capitol Park and Planning Commission. File copy.

261. Courant. 1865. June 13. James O. Hall Research Center. Maryland-National Capitol Park and Planning Commission. File copy.

262. The *Courant.* 1865. June 16. James O. Hall Research Center. Maryland-National Capitol Park and Planning Commission. File copy.

263. Steers, E., Jr. and H. Holzer, eds. 2009. The Lincoln Assassination Conspirators Their Confinement and Execution As Recorded in the Letterbook of John Hartranft. Louisiana State University Press. Baton Rouge. 179 pp.

264. Surratt, J.H. 1870. Lecture at Rockville, Maryland. Transcript carried in December 7, 1870 edition of the *Evening Star* newspaper, Washington, D.C.

265. Lee, E.G. 1865. Diary of Edwin Gray Lee. Unpublished microfilm. James O. Hall Research Center. File copy.

266. Ibid.

267. Ibid.

268. Fisher, G.P. Hon. Presiding. 1867. Trial of John H. Surratt in the Criminal Court for the District of Columbia. Washington Government Printing Office. Testimony of Boucher. 678 pp.

269. Lee, E.G. 1865. Diary of Edwin Gray Lee.

270. Ibid.

Fearless, Lewis Powell was the first made ready of the four to be hanged; Mary Surratt is still seated. Library of Congress, LC-DIG-cwpb-04229.

Alexander Gardner's photograph captured (within capability of the technology of that day) exaggerated swinging immediately after the drop resulting from the conspirators being incorrectly positioned on the trap. Library of Congress, LC-DIG-ppmsca-35256.

CHAPTER FIFTEEN

Jury of Peers

June 1867

John Surratt left Canada in September 1865 and, using his Catholic connections, landed a job half a world away in Rome as a member of the Vatican Guard. But in November of 1866 he was identified, arrested and held for extradition to the United States. Yet he managed to escape while being relocated to Rome by his former brothers in arms and fled to Egypt, where he was nabbed again and returned to Washington.

On June 10, 1867, Surratt was on trial for his role in the assassination of Abraham Lincoln. Nettie Gilbert (she was again using her maiden name) had divorced Rowan Slater by then and lived in New York City. She read the newspapers and knew that Surratt was in U.S. custody. Would she too be arrested and charged?

Two years earlier, Surratt had boarded the steamer *Peruvian* in Quebec City and left for freedom in Europe. But during the crossing he made a foolish mistake. He told the ship's surgeon, with whom he was sharing a room, about his work as a Confederate spy and Lincoln conspirator. This eventually led to Surratt's arrest in Rome.

But unlike his mother and the others, he was tried in a U.S. civilian court. Military trials of civilians were generally no longer allowed in federal districts with functioning civilian courts thanks to an 1866 Supreme Court ruling known as *Ex Parte Milligan*. John Surratt was tried by a jury of his peers, and Washington was populated by many people who maintained Confederate sympathies.

Nettie Gilbert surely followed Surratt's trial as the story unfolded. If the government failed in its prosecution of him, other conspirators still at large—including former Confederate spies Thomas Harbin and Mrs. Slater—were not likely to be at further risk.

The prosecution called Louis Weichmann.

Question: "I will come to the 25th of March 1865. Did you see John Surratt on that day?"

Weichmann: "Yes sir. As I went to breakfast and looked out of the dining-room window, I saw John Surratt, his mother and Mrs. Slater, who had been at the house previously, in a carriage containing four seats, to which were attached a pair of white horses."

Question: "Do you know where the horses came from?"

Weichmann: "Yes sir. Mrs. Surratt, the same evening, told me that the horses had been hired from Brooke Stabler."

Question: "Did the three go away together?"

Weichmann: "Yes sir."

Question: "About what time of day did the three leave?"

Weichmann: "About 8 o'clock in the morning."

Question: "When did you next see Mrs. Surratt?"

Weichmann: "I saw her the same evening."

Question: "Where?"

Weichmann: "In her house."

Question: "Did Mrs. Slater and John Surratt return with her?"

Weichmann: "No sir."

Question: "Did Mrs. Surratt tell you anything that occurred with them?"

Weichmann: "I asked where John had gone. She said he had gone to Richmond with Mrs. Slater to get a clerkship."[271]

Next, John Surratt's lawyer, Joseph Habersham Bradley, cross-examined Weichmann, picking at the details to find contradictions. He frustrated Weichmann but never broke him. Bradley focused on Surratt's travel to New York in early February 1865 but said nothing about his client first going to Canada and returning to Washington City to escort Mrs. Slater.

Question: "Don't you know what he went for?"

Answer: "No sir."

Question: "Didn't he tell you he went there to see a lady and bring her back home with him?"

Answer: "A lady did come back with him."

Question: "Did he tell you he went there for that purpose?"

Answer: "Not that I remember."

Question: "You do not remember that?"

Answer: "No sir. I do not remember that particular circumstance."

Question: "Where was it that he told you he had seen Booth, and that Booth had an elegant home there?"

Answer: "In his own house."

Question: "When?"

Answer: "After he got back."

Question: "How long?"

Answer: "A few days."

Question: "How many days?"

Answer: "I do not know."

Question: "Ten days or a week?"

Answer: "I do not know the day, hour and minute of everything."[272]

Defense attorney Bradley pressed the frustrated witness, saying: "You have testified to so many dates, and with such particularity, that I want to see how much you remember about others. It is not my suggestion; it is yours."

Weichmann understood what Bradley was getting at. The cross examination was not about discovering the truth. It was about discrediting Weichmann.

Question: "On that occasion when John Surratt went to New York and brought a lady back, you did not see her at all?"

Weichmann: "No sir."

Question: "Did she arrive in the afternoon?"

Weichmann: "Yes sir."

Question: "How do you know, if you didn't see her at all?"

Weichmann: "Well, I know it from circumstances."

Question: "Will you describe how she was dressed at the time she first came?"

Weichmann: "I do not know how she was dressed at the time I first saw her. I know she had one of those small veils over the face, which came down to the chin."

Question: "When was that?"

Weichmann: "That was sometime in March."[273]

Bradley then rolled out testimony Weichmann gave two years previously in the trial of the conspirators in which he said that Mrs. Slater wore a mask.

Weichmann responded: "I do not remember saying so; I may have done so. What I intended to say now was that Mrs. Slater did not wear any disguise. I understood you to have referenced something to conceal the face. I remember I did use the word 'mask.'"[274]

Bradley concluded his questioning and Weichmann was not recalled. The public never forgave Weichmann for his role in the execution of Mary Surratt. Critics described her hanging as "judicial murder," and the U.S. Supreme Court gave credence to it with a subsequent ruling against future military tribunals involving civilians. Weichmann had been honest but was tormented over his motives in saving himself over Mary Surratt. He worked to justify his actions and defend his honor until the day he died in 1902.

The prosecution next called ship's surgeon Dr. Lewis J.A. McMillan to the stand.

Question: "What ship are you connected with?

McMillan: "From April till October 1865, I was surgeon of the steamship *Peruvian*."

He was then directed to proceed in narrative form:

"I remember his (Surratt) stating that he at one time was told in Montreal that he would meet a lady in New York … that he met the woman in New York; he came on to Washington with her; from Washington he started on the way to Richmond with her and four or five others; that after a great deal of trouble, they managed to cross the Potomac; that after they got south of Fredericksburg, they were driven on a platform car drawn or pushed by Negroes. As they were drawn along, they saw some men coming towards them—five or six, if I recollect right. They ascertained that these men were Union prisoners, or Union soldiers escaped from Southern prisons; they were, he said, nearly starved to death; that this woman who was with them said, 'Let's shoot the damned Yankee soldiers.' She had hardly said the word when they all drew their revolvers and shot them and went right along paying no more attention to them."

Question: "Did he tell you the name of this woman?"

McMillan: "He did, but I forget at this distance of time. I could not positively state who she was."

Question: "Would you know the name if you were to hear it?"

McMillan: "I would not like to say now what it was."

Question: "Do you know what letter of the alphabet it commenced with?"

McMillan: "I could not say."

Question: "Was the name Mrs. Slater?"

McMillan: "It sounds like it, but I would not be positive that it is. The woman's name was very conspicuous in Montreal during the trial of the St. Albans raiders."

Question: "Conspicuous as what?"

McMillan: "As one of those who went to Richmond to help the raiders in their trial."

Question: Did he (Surratt) give you any account of crossing the Potomac at that time? If so, state it.

McMillan: "I remember his stating … there were several of them crossing the Potomac in a boat—it was in the evening, I believe—when they were perceived by a gunboat and hailed. They were ordered to surrender. The gunboat sent a small boat to them; that they waited until the gunboat came immediately alongside them, then fired right into them, and escaped to the shore."

Question: "In passing between Richmond, Washington and Montreal, did he state anything of the names he took? And, if so, give them."

McMillan: "I remember that he traveled under the names Harrison, Sherman and some others I forget."

Question: "Did he tell you what he received and from whom he received it?"

McMillan: "He stated that he received a letter from John Wilkes Booth, dated 'New York' ordering him immediately to Washington, as it had been necessary for them to change their plans, and to act promptly."

John Surratt was in Montreal April 6-12 before leaving on the Elmira mission for Confederate department chief E.G. Lee. The City of Montreal and these April dates provide the only location and times when and where Surratt could have received this message of changed plans.

Booth was in New York City on April 7, having traveled there following his romantic getaway with Lucy Hale at the Aquidneck House in Rhode Island three days earlier. It was on April 7 in New York City that Booth boasted to his friend, Sam Chester, "What an excellent chance I had to kill the President, if I had wished, on Inauguration Day."

En route to Montreal from Washington, Surratt stopped on April 5 at Edwin Booth's house hoping to find his brother, John Wilkes Booth. But Surratt did not wait around and proceeded to Montreal.

During Surratt's trial, the questioning of Dr. McMillan turned to Montreal, where John had fled after he heard about the assassination.

Question: "Did he tell you to whose house he went?"

McMillan: "He told me that he went to one Mr. Porterfield's in Montreal."

Question: "Did he tell you who he (Porterfield) was?"

McMillan: "He told me Mr. Porterfield was a Confederate agent in Montreal."

Question: "What did he tell you as occurring there to himself?"

McMillan: "He said he stayed there a short time; how long I would not say; until, however, they found out that detectives were beginning to suspect that he was in the house, and it was found necessary for him to leave there."

McMillan: "Did he tell you how he left there?"

Answer: "He said that one evening two carriages were driven in front of Mr. Porterfield's house; and that he and another party dressed nearly as he was came out at the same time, and one got into one carriage, and the other one in the other, and drove off; one carriage driving one way and the other in the other."

During the cross-examination the next day, actions of Nettie Slater again came up.

Question: "I understood you to say yesterday that he (Surratt) said when he was going down below Fredericksburg, on a car driven by Negroes and in company with a lady, that some men came along, and the lady said, 'Shoot the damned Yankees," and there upon they fired into them and left them on the ground.

McMillan: "I think that he said, 'fired at them' and left them on the ground and went on their way. I would not positively say that he used the words 'on the ground.'"

Question: "What induced you to make the affidavit as soon as you landed?"

McMillan: "Because I thought the prisoner was guilty of a crime not only against our society, but against civilization. I thought it was my duty as a man to go and give him up to the proper authorities."[275]

It's important to note that, by the time John Surratt was on trial, public sympathy for his executed mother had spread and, as a result, prosecution of another woman in the case was unlikely. But Dr. McMillan's testimony specifically mentioned that a female conspirator had called for the murders of federal soldiers who had been walking along some railroad tracks. Surely, the former Nettie Slater, now Gilbert, was well aware of the implications of that testimony as she read the New York newspaper accounts of Surratt's trial.

Defense attorney Bradley failed to fully contradict the prosecution's witnesses as he had hoped, but he did sow seeds of reasonable doubt in the minds of jurors, eight of whom were Southerners. Indeed, all eight of them voted to acquit Surratt. The others decided he was guilty.

Surratt was returned to jail to await a second trial—which never happened. The prosecution had done a poor job, and it occurred two years after Lincoln's murder. Four people had already been hanged for the crime, and one was a woman who many people thought should have been spared. The public generally lost interest in the case, and the government got tangled in technicalities. As of December 1868, no indictments remained against John Harrison Surratt—and he was a free man.

The former Nettie Slater surely breathed a sigh of relief.

Literature Cited – Chapter 15

271. Fisher, G.P. 1867. Trial of John H. Surratt in the Criminal Court for the District of Columbia, Hon. George P. Fisher Presiding. Vol. 1. Testimony of L. J. Weichmann. Government Printing Office. Washington D.C. 678 pp.

272. Ibid.

273. Ibid.

274. Ibid.

275. Fisher, G.P. 1867. Trial of John H. Surratt in the Criminal Court for the District of Columbia, Hon. George P. Fisher Presiding. Vol. 1. Testimony of L. J. A. McMillan. Government Printing Office. Washington D.C. 678 pp.

CHAPTER SIXTEEN

War Under the Black Flag

FEBRUARY–SEPTEMBER 1864

THE YEAR 1864 arrived as a year of desperation for authorities in both the north and south. Abraham Lincoln's popularity could not fall any lower, re-election was barely a hope. Even a member of his own cabinet was plotting a run against him. A negotiated peace would most likely leave his nation divided. One hundred miles south in Richmond, Jefferson Davis struggled to resuscitate a crippled economy and find the wherewithal—money and men—to sustain his rebellion. Desperate men were about to do desperate things.

Union General Judson Kilpatrick earned a moniker from the troops under his command—although "Kill-Cavalry" was no compliment. Even so, he was Lincoln's kind of general. Judson Kilpatrick was not hesitant to engage the enemy and fight.

On February 11, 1864, Kilpatrick took a plan directly to the president and told Lincoln that he could slip his cavalry around the right flank of Lee's Army of Northern Virginia—firmly in place on the south bank of the Rappahannock River—and into Richmond. U.S. cavalrymen had previously advanced to within striking distance of the city before being turned back, and Kilpatrick vowed they could do it again.[276]

Once south of Fredericksburg and behind Lee's lines, the federal cavalry would face little or no resistance from advancing on Richmond, the president was told. The attacking force would separate into two units, Kilpatrick said, and he would personally lead the charge of almost 3,500 men into the city from the north. He said a smaller and faster unit—500 cavalrymen strong—would ride south and west, and ford the James River upstream of Richmond, then ride east before striking back across the river into lightly defended Richmond from the south. Success depended on well-coordinated attacks by both cavalry units in a pincer movement that would trap the Confederacy's leaders and end the war.

Col. Ulric Dahlgren, a young and charismatic U.S. cavalry officer who lost a leg outside Gettysburg, had convalesced in Washington, knew President Lincoln and wanted back in the fight.[277] So Lincoln told Kilpatrick that he approved the plan on the condition that Col. Dahlgren was allowed to lead the smaller cavalry unit south of Richmond. Kilpatrick agreed.

February weather in Virginia is typically cold and wet. But 1864 was an exception: It was unusually dry and dusty. J.B. Jones, a thin and aging clerk who worked in the Confederate War Department, noted in his journal the clouds of dust he stirred with each step he took across one of Richmond's main streets. Add a multitude of people, horses and wagons, and the city was filthy, he wrote. There had only been one significant rain all winter,[278] yielding conditions ideal for a wintertime military campaign.

On February 28, Union raiders crossed the Rappahannock River, rode south of Fredericksburg and slipped behind Gen. Lee's lines. A light rain fell early the next day, and by nightfall on March 1 the advancing cavalry was drenched from rains that turned heavy.[279]

Despite the rain and his wooden leg, Col. Dahlgren handled himself well in his saddle. He and his men rode hard and fast to cover the longer distance they had to travel—almost 75 miles compared to Gen. Kilpatrick's 50. The attacks were to be launched simultaneously from north and south of Richmond. Col. Dahlgren fully understood the importance of the timing but delayed his movement long enough to attack the plantation home of Confederate Secretary of War James Seddon.

Before the end of the day, rumors of the capture of Seddon's family members had reached clerk J.B. Jones in Richmond.[280] Word moved along the Confederate grapevine faster than the advance of the Union cavalry. Col. Dahlgren's decision to delay his movement in order to assault a non-military target was not only pointless but led to a Yankee disaster.

After the plantation raid, Martin Robinson, a free Black man, risked his life to guide Col. Dahlgren and his men to a certain ford across the James River upstream from Richmond. But after two days of rain, the river was too swollen to cross on horseback. Stuck north of the river and running out of time, the impetuous colonel assumed he had been betrayed and ordered the hanging of Robinson on the spot.

Dahlgren then turned east toward Richmond without crossing the river in a failed attempt to join Gen. Kilpatrick's main thrust from the north. On the evening of March 2, the city's home guard—which included government clerks, many of whom were veteran soldiers no longer capable of regular field service—were well led and prepared to defend the city.[281] One unit on the outskirts east of the city were ordered to lie flat on the ground in the darkness and rain and hold their fire until the Union cavalry was within 15 yards of their line. At that moment the signal to stand and fire was given, and the Rebels unleashed a withering volley on the enemy. Dahlgren was hit multiple times and fell dead from his saddle. What was left of his troop turned and fled. Many were captured.

The defenders found in the dead colonel's pockets two documents: orders for the raid and a speech to his troops written in Dahlgren's own hand. The information documented an irregular warfare action against civilians that virtually all Southerners and many Northerners considered illegal and immoral, and easily traced back to the President of the United States.

The papers made clear that a proposed objective of the raid—freeing Union soldiers imprisoned at Belle Island in the James River—was legitimate and within the rules of war. But the main objective was to attack Richmond and burn the "hateful" city. The third objective was shocking: "The men must be kept together and well in hand, and, once in the city it must be destroyed, and Jeff Davis and his cabinet killed."[282] Also, in the aftermath of the failed raid, captured federal troops possessed incendiaries in quantities enough to set Richmond ablaze.

Within two days, the unvarnished story of Dahlgren's failed attack was published in the *Richmond Examiner* and the *Richmond Sentinel*, and editorials calling for retribution soon followed. Clandestine operations need to be invisible; covert operations require a measure of deniability. Irregular warfare by federal military units inflicted on nontraditional targets lacked both characteristics. Winning at all costs had become the bottom line in 1864. The newspapers called it "War under the Black Flag."

Not long after Kilpatrick's failed attack on Richmond, Confederate Gen. Robert E. Lee wrote a letter to Union Gen. George Meade asking if Col. Dahlgren's actions reflected a new policy regarding the United States' conduct of the war. Lee sent his letter and copies of the captured documentation across the lines under a flag of truce.

Gen. Meade's response was unambiguous. "In reply, I have to state that neither the United States government, myself nor Gen. Kilpatrick authorized, sanctioned or approved the burning of the city of Richmond and the killing of Mr. Davis and cabinet."[283]

But Meade did not contest the legitimacy of Lee's documentation. Neither did Lincoln. Perhaps Meade was unaware that Lincoln had approved Kilpatrick's raid. It was no secret that Meade's hesitancy to send his men into combat had raised Lincoln's ire. The two were not close. Either President Lincoln sanctioned the killing of President Jefferson Davis and members of his cabinet or Col. Dahlgren had determined in advance to do so on his own.

Young Dahlgren was raised in a military family and fully indoctrinated in rules regarding the chain of command. He and his father, U.S. Navy Adm. John Dahlgren, rose to high ranks within that culture. In addition, Col. Dahlgren owed a personal debt of gratitude to Lincoln for getting him back into the war. So the question is, after receiving his new and coveted command, did the young colonel announce to his troops the entirety of their orders, which would have set national policy at variance with wishes of the Commander and Chief regarding conduct of the war?

This is highly unlikely. In November 1862, Lincoln relieved Gen.

Benjamin "the Beast" Butler for actions contrary to national policy. And when he complained, Butler heard: "The reason was one which does not imply, on the part of the government, any want of confidence in your honor as a man or your ability as a commander."[284] In June 1863, Gen. David Hunter ordered the burning of Darien, Ga. and was relieved of his command a day later. When he complained to Lincoln, the president replied by letter: "I assure you, and you may feel authorized in stating, that the recent change of commanders in the Department of the South was made for no reasons which convey any imputation upon your known energy, efficiency and patriotism; but for causes which seemed sufficient, while they were in no degree incompatible with the respect and esteem in which I have always held you as a man and an officer."[285]

It was no secret that Lincoln had previously relieved Gens. Hunter and Butler of their commands for actions contrary to national policy and felt no obligation to justify his decision. There is no reason to conclude that the president's attitude had changed on that score.

In the fallout of the Kilpatrick-Dahlgren raid, Southerners were disinclined to believe Northern denials regarding federal government's policy. They did not have to wait long for confirmation of their misgivings. Before the end of spring, black flag warfare was documented in the orders given by Union major generals and in associated actions by troops in the field under their commands. It was documented in orders given by Jefferson Davis, too. Leaders within the Confederate government did not wait to see with their own eyes what they already believed. The Rebels had irregular actions underway well before the end of spring. Now it would be a proverbial eye for an eye, maybe more.

Jefferson Davis identified one of two men to assist the Confederacy in secret service. He sent a telegram to fellow Mississippian Jacob Thompson. "If your engagements permit you to accept service abroad for the next six months, please come here immediately."[286,287] Thompson was wealthy and quite sharp regarding money matters. Before the war he was a U.S. congressman and later served as President James Buchanan's secretary of the interior. He brought excellent credentials to the Confederacy when he answered the call to serve his new country. President Davis wanted Thompson to work with Clement Clay of Alabama to lead the Confederacy's Department of the North in Canada. Davis also wrote to Clay:

> *"Confiding special trust in your zeal, discretion and patriotism, I hereby direct you to proceed to Canada, there to carry out such instructions as you have received from me verbally, in such manner as shall seem most likely to conduce to the furtherance of the interests of the Confederate States of America which have been entrusted to you."*[288]

Specifically, President Davis wanted his two commissioners to "inaugurate certain hostile movements in Northern territory." Their first challenge was to get to Canada.

Closer to Richmond, Confederate spies were on the move. They watched and noted the comings and goings of the President of the United States. It was about that time when Col. Bradley Johnson proposed using Confederate cavalry for kidnapping Lincoln during one of the president's regular visits to the Soldiers Home just outside the city. Lincoln often went there unguarded.[289]

This was not the first time that Jefferson Davis heard such a proposal. Two years earlier, Joseph Taylor, a cousin of the Davis' first wife, Sarah Knox, told the Confederate president that it was possible to kidnap Lincoln in route to the Soldiers Home. "No sir," Davis told Taylor. "I will not give my authority to abduct Lincoln."[290]

Davis had heard more extreme proposals regarding Lincoln. In 1861, a man named C.L.V. De Kalb wrote then-Confederate Secretary of War Leroy Pope Walker the following:

> *"Does the Southern Confederacy consider the explosion of the federal Capitol, at a time when Abe, his Myrmidons and the Northern Congress members all are assembled together, of sufficient importance as to grant me, in case of success, a commission of colonel of topographical engineers, and the sum of one million dollars?"*[291]

In 1863, a man named H.C. Durham proposed the assassinations of Northern leaders "Seward, Lincoln, Greeley, Prentice, etc." But such proposals for lethal, irregular warfare were readily declined during the early war years.

However, all of this changed when the United States and the Confederate States descended into total war. On July 17, 1864, following a retreat with his Union Army of the Shenandoah to Charles Town, Virginia, Maj. Gen. David Hunter ordered the arrest of his elderly cousin Andrew Hunter, a civilian and Confederate sympathizer, and jailed him for a month under a nationwide suspension of a writ of habeas corpus that Lincoln had imposed since Sept. 25, 1862.[292] Hunter also ordered his cousin's house burned to the ground.

Hunter never offered justification for destroying his Southern cousin's property. Perhaps it related to Andrew Hunter's role in supporting prosecutors in John Brown's trial. This included a speech he gave on behalf of the Commonwealth of Virginia in which he challenged the value of an alliance with Northern states. In a reference to the burning of buildings, he asked, "... did that bond of Union—which may ultimately prove a bad bond to us in the South—allow him (Brown) to come into the bosom of the Commonwealth with the deadly purpose of applying the torch to our buildings and shedding the blood of our citizens?"[293] Given his cousin's history of posturing for the South, perhaps Gen. Hunter's action was based on contempt for a member of his own family.

Two homes in Shepherdstown became Gen. Hunter's next targets. The first belonged to his cousin, Mrs. Alexander Boteler. One of the Hunter's officers displayed the General's orders before his men plundered the woman's belongings. Next, they drenched the house in kerosene and ignited the blaze as Mrs. Boteler's two daughters and three grandchildren watched the place burn.

The home of civilian Edmund Jennings Lee II was also burned to the ground. Lee was not there at the time but his wife, Henrietta, his daughter and youngest son were. Henrietta was the mother of Confederate (then Colonel) Gen. Edwin Gray Lee and a cousin by marriage of Gen. Robert E. Lee. Henrietta confronted the Union officer who was in charge of the atrocity and challenged him not to execute what she described as Hunter's "barbarous, infamous order." The officer scoffed, called Henrietta a fool and fired the house and outbuildings. Henrietta later wrote a letter to Gen. Hunter:

"JEFFERSON COUNTY, July 20, 1864

General Hunter:
Yesterday your underling Captain Martindale, of the First New York cavalry, executed your infamous order and burned my house. You have had the satisfaction ere this of receiving from him the information that your orders were fulfilled to the letter; the dwelling with every out-building, seven in number, with their contents, being burned. I, therefore, a helpless woman whom you have cruelly wronged, address you, a Major General of the United States Army, and demand to know why was this done? What was my offence? My husband was absent, an exile. He has never been a politician or in any way engaged in the struggle now going on, his age preventing. This fact, your Chief of Staff, David Strother, could have told you. The house was built by my father, a Revolutionary soldier, who served the whole seven years for your independence. There I was born; there the sacred dead repose. It was my house and my home, and there your niece, Miss Griffith, who has tarried among us all this horrid war up to the present time, met with all kindness and hospitality at my hands. Was it for this that you have turned me, my young daughter and little son out upon the world without a shelter? Or was it because my husband is the grandson of the Revolutionary patriot and 'rebel' Richard Henry Lee, and the near kinsman of the noblest of Christian warriors, the greatest of Generals, Robert E. Lee? Heaven's blessing be upon his head forever. You and your Government have failed to conquer, subdue or match him; and disappointment, rage and malice find vent on the helpless and inoffensive.

"Hyena like, you have torn my heart to pieces! For all hallowed memories clustered round that homestead, and demon-like, you have done it without even the pretext of revenge, for I never saw you or harmed you. Your office is not to lead, like a brave man and soldier, your men to fight in the ranks of war, but your work has been to separate yourself from all danger, and with your incendiary band steal unawares upon helpless women and children, to insult and destroy. Two fair homes did you yesterday

ruthlessly lay in ashes, giving not a moment's warning to the startled inmates of your wicked purpose; turning mothers and children out of doors, you are execrated by your own men for the cruel work you gave them to do.

"In the case of Colonel A. R. Boteler, both father and mother were far away. Any heart but of Captain Martindale and yours would have been touched by that little circle, comprising a widowed daughter just risen from her bed of illness, her three fatherless babies—the oldest not five years old—and her heroic sister. I repeat, any man would have been touched at that sight but Captain Martindale. One might as well hope to find mercy and feeling in the heart of a wolf bent on his prey of young lambs, as to search for such qualities in his bosom. You have chosen well your agent for such deeds, and doubtless will promote him!

"A colonel of the Federal army has stated that you have deprived forty of your officers of their commands because they would not carry out your malignant mischief. All honor to their names for this at least! They are men—they have human hearts and blush for such a commander!

"I ask who that does not wish infamy and disgrace attached to his name forever would serve under you? Your name will stand on history's page as the Hunter of weak women and innocent children; the Hunter to destroy defenseless villages and refined and beautiful homes—to torture afresh the agonized hearts of suffering widows; the Hunter of Africa's poor sons and daughters to lure them to ruin and death of soul and body; the Hunter with the relentless heart of a wild beast, the face of a fiend and the form of a man. O Earth, behold the Monster! Can I say 'God forgive you?' No prayer can be offered for you! Were it possible for human lips to raise your name heavenward, angels would thrust the foul thing back again, and demons claim their own. The curses of thousands, the scorn of the manly and upright and the hatred of the true and honorable, will follow you and yours through all time, and brand upon your name infamy! Infamy!

"Again, I demand why have you burned my house? Answer as you must answer before the Searcher of all hearts, why have you added this cruel, wicked deed to your many crimes?

Henrietta E. Lee"[294]

The Richmond *Enquirer*, the Philadelphia *Bulletin*, the Liverpool *Courier* and various other periodicals printed Mrs. Lee's letter. By November 8, the New York *Express* reprinted it. The personality of the War of the Rebellion was hardening in 1864, and everyone knew it.

Mrs. Lee's letter received minor editorial changes just prior, and likely during, the publications of 1864 and, perhaps, in later printings. In an earlier version, some minor changes in grammar and punctuation were added by Henrietta Lee's oldest son, Edwin Gray Lee.

Her curse on Gen. Hunter was exquisite. Her reference to "Africa's sons and daughters" referenced a previous order by Hunter when, as commander of the U.S. Department of the South, he issued his own emancipation proclamation months prior to that by Abraham Lincoln. Hunter's order horrified Southern planters who feared slave revolts, and it soon became unpopular with slaves because afterwards he impressed them into military service.[295] Many considered it trading one form of servitude for another.

The Confederacy, which did not have soldiers in the North and available for irregular warfare, did plan a response. Secretary of War James Seddon ordered one of the South's best spies, Thomas Conrad, to go back to Washington City on a special assignment.

Conrad had to be careful. Because he was known by some federal detectives as a Southern sympathizer, his strategy was to dress and act in such a way as to hide in plain sight. He avoided hotel lobbies, restaurants and barrooms, and attended Catholic masses where no one knew him except for the priest.[296] Conrad was familiar with the Old Capitol Prison, which was at a corner of First and A streets in the rear of the Capitol. It was a three-story, brick building that held citizens accused of various offenses, often unspecified, against the U.S. government.[297]

Conrad himself had been held there for several summer days for relatively minor acts of disloyalty. While an instructor at Georgetown College, he was accused of having a music instructor play "Dixie" at the close of 1861 graduation ceremonies.

During this mission, Conrad operated from his base at "Castle Green," also known as the Van Ness mansion.[298] It was a fine brick house owned by

Tom and Nannie Green, who had ties with covert Confederate agents in southern Maryland. Partition walls of the house ran to some depth to cellars. A trap door accessed one of the cellars, which was an ideal hiding place if need be.[299]

Conrad spent hours watching the White House from Lafayette Square, a reasonable walk from Castle Green. He noted the times, dates, days of the week, weather and company associated with Lincoln's travels. The President typically left for a visit to the Soldiers Home on pleasantly cool evenings, sometimes accompanied by others inside his private carriage. Lincoln never had armed escorts on these trip, and always drove out 14th Street to Columbia Road. Conrad and friend Edward Norton—who happened to be a federal detective in Washington City—planned to follow the carriage closely as the road cut through woods to the Soldiers Home. It was there that the third team member was to halt carriage while the others moved in on Lincoln.

Conrad knew in advance that he had support from Confederate Col. John S. Mosby—The Grey Ghost—and Lt. Charles Cawood, who operated the Confederate signal station moving mail and certain people across the Potomac. On September 15, 1864, Confederate Secretary of War James Seddon signed orders: "Lt. Col. Mosby and Lieutenant Cawood are hereby directed to aid and facilitate the movements of Capt. Conrad."[300]

If the kidnappers got Lincoln to the Potomac River, the Confederacy would have their man prior to his run for re-election. But someone within the administration finally convinced Lincoln to add a cavalry escort on such trips.

And, of course, the idea of total war was fully carried out by Gen. William T. Sherman on his fiery and devastating march across Georgia to Savannah, the city that he offered to Lincoln as a Christmas present at the end of that year. Sherman, then moving north through South Carolina, was isolated. This gave Gen. Robert E. Lee a tempting prize—but only if Lee could steal a march away from Grant and reach the Carolinas.

Literature Cited – Chapter 16

276. Steers, E., Jr. 2001. Blood on the Moon. The University Press of Kentucky. Lexington, Kentucky. 360 pp.

277. Ibid.

278. Jones, J.B. 1866. A Rebel War Clerks Diary. J.B. Lippincott & Co. Philadelphia, Pennsylvania. 482 pp.

279. Ibid.

280. Ibid.

281. Steers, E., Jr. 2001.

282. Headley, J.W., Captain C. S. A. 1906. Confederate Operations in Canada and New York. The Neale Publishing Company.

283. Steers, E., Jr. 2001.

284. Butler, B.F. 1892. Butler's Book. A.M. Thayer & Co. Boston, Ma. 1166 pp.

285. Lincoln, A. 1863. Letter to General David Hunter of June 30th. Collected Works of Abraham Lincoln, Vol. 6. University of Michigan Digital Library. 580 pp.

286. Headley, J.W., Captain C. S. A. 1906.

287. Cameron, S.F. (presumed author). Date unspecified. Untitled Manuscript, Notes for a "History of the Confederate Secret Service." Unpublished. James O. Hall Research Center. Maryland-National Capital Park and Planning Commission. File copy. 25 pp.

288. Boutwell, G.S. 1866. Assassination of Lincoln. Report of House of Representatives. No. 104. 41 pp.

289. Steers, E., Jr. 2001.

290. Louthan, H.T. 1908. "A Proposed Abduction of Lincoln." Confederate Veteran. 434 pp.

291. Boutwell, G.S. 1866.

292. Lincoln, A. 1862. General Orders No. 141. Gilder Lehrman Collection.

293. Hunter, A. 1859. Speech as recorded. The Life, Trial and Execution of Captain John Brown Known as "Old Brown of Osawatomie," With a Full Account of the Attempted Insurrection at Harper's Ferry. Robert M. DeWitt Publisher. New York, New York.

294. Lee, H.E. 1864. Letter to General David Hunter of July 20th. Southern Historical Society Papers, Vol. 8. Richmond, Virginia. Published 1882. Digitized by Google. 607 pp.

295. Lincoln, A. 1862. Presidential Proclamation No. 90. National Archives. Series 23, Record Group 11.

296. Conrad, T., Captain C.S.A. 1904. The Rebel Scout. The National Publishing Company. Washington City. 232 pp.

297. Ibid.

298. Ibid.

299. Oldroyd, O. H. 1901. The Assassination of Abraham Lincoln. Private printing, Washington D.C. 364 pp.

300. Conrad, T.N, Captain C.S.A. 1892. A Confederate Spy. J. S. Ogilvie Publisher. New York, New York. Digitized by Google. 142 pp.

General Judson Kilpatrick's failed cavalry raid against Richmond signaled the beginning of the total war of 1864. Library of Congress. LC-BH82-4141.

General David Hunter, infamous across the South, headed the military tribunal that tried eight Lincoln conspirators. Civil War Photographs, 1861–1865, Library of Congress, Brady portraits.

Col. Ulric Dahlgren (standing) was photographed with other Union officers one month before losing a leg in the Gettysburg campaign. During the cavalry raid on Richmond the following February, he carried documentation of a new phase of warfare against the southern states.

General Robert E. Lee sent copies of the papers removed from Colonel Dahlgren's pockets to United States General George Meade requesting clarification regarding federal policy in future conduct of the war. Library of Congress, Prints and Photographs Division, cwpb.04402.

General George Meade responded to General Lee's inquiry stating that neither the United States government, he, nor General Kilpatrick approved the burning of Richmond and killing Jefferson Davis. General Meade offered no challenge to the authenticity of General Lee's documentation. Library of Congress, LC-DIG-cwpbh-01198.

EPILOGUE

Mrs. Spencer

1870–1920

SARAH ANTOINETTE SPENCER's health was failing on April 8, 1920 in Poughkeepsie, New York when she signed her last will and testament. She had been married three times and experienced one divorce—and outlived all of her husbands. Her first was dancing master and Confederate soldier, Rowan Slater, and the other two were Union veterans. None of them likely knew details about her brief career as a Confederate spy, and the U.S. government had long since quit caring about her role in the assassination of the nation's 16th president.

Some of her Confederate colleagues wrote about their adventures as undercover agents during the great struggle between the North and the South. But Mrs. Spencer kept most of her story to herself—including her actual age. Had it been what she claimed, the former Nettie Gilbert would have been 10 years old when John Wilkes Booth shot Abraham Lincoln.

Louis Weichmann's self-tortured life ended in 1902. While he didn't lie to detectives or in his testimony, he never got over willingly offering up Mary Surratt to save his own neck. Much of his time and energy was dedicated to defending his honor to a public that thought that Mrs. Surratt was a victim of judicial murder.

John Harrison Surratt died in 1916, never once expressing regrets for his actions. Others were to blame for Lincoln's murder and his mother's execution—always—in Surratt's mind.

Mrs. Slater's other Confederate escorts—James Fowle and Augustus Spencer Howell—died soon after the war, which took a heavy toll on their health as it did many others.

Secret service chief Edwin Gray Lee died of tuberculosis in 1870 in Virginia. He was called to testify in Washington in the trial of John Surratt in 1867 but offered little evidence due to legal wrangling and objections over the leading questions asked of him. His disease robbed him of vitality and his post-war years were much about seeking relief for his damaged lungs.

Confederate spy Stephen F. Cameron died of tuberculosis in 1878 before he could finish his book about of his secret service. After the war, Cameron returned to Catholicism, and he was buried in Brooklyn, New York.

Agent Thomas Harbin, of the Confederate Signal Corps, passed away in 1885, and was buried in Mount Olivet Cemetery in Washington, as was Mary Surratt.

Confederate spy Thomas Nelson Conrad—who wrote about his covert activities during the war—became president of Virginia Agricultural and Mechanical College, which later became Virginia Polytechnic Institute and State University, and today is Virginia Tech University in Blacksburg. He died in Washington in 1905.

Nettie outlived all of them, passing away on June 20, 1920 from chronic kidney disease two months after signing her will.[301] She had no children and no debt. She left what was left of her modest estate to nieces, nephews and friends.[302] The wealth of her secrets about her life as a Confederate spy were left with no one. Her intelligence and skills protected her during the war and her self-discipline did so during years that followed.

Some of her secrets are included in this book; most are yet to be recorded in American history—if ever.

Literature Cited – Epilogue

301. New York State Division of Vital Statistics. 1920. Standard Certificate of Death. Sarah A. Spencer.

302. Spencer, S. A. 1920. Will and Probate File. Surrogate's Court, Dutchess County, New York.